Liturgy
Documentary
Series

Lectionary for Mass

Second Typical
Edition
Introduction

United States Catholic Conference
Washington, D.C.

In its 1998 planning document, as approved by the general membership of the National Conference of Catholic Bishops, the Secretariat of the NCCB Committee on the Liturgy was authorized to revise and update Secretariat publications. The revised edition of *Liturgy Documentary Series 1: Lectionary for Mass: Introduction* was approved by Archbishop Jerome G. Hanus, OSB, chairman of the NCCB Committee on the Liturgy, and authorized for publication by the undersigned.

Monsignor Dennis M. Schnurr
General Secretary
NCCB/USCC

First printing, October 1998

ISBN 1-57455-245-7

CONTENTS

FOREWORD

On the night before he died, Christ gathered with his disciples to celebrate the Last Supper. There, he took bread and wine and gave it to them as the everlasting sign of the new covenant in his blood (Lk 22:20). From that night onward, "the Church has never ceased to celebrate his paschal mystery by coming together to read what referred to him in all the Scriptures (Lk 24:27), and to carry out the work of salvation through the celebration of the memorial of the Lord and through the sacraments" (*Lectionary for Mass* [LFM], no. 10).

In the earliest days of the Church, the apostles gathered weekly for "the breaking of the bread and the prayers" (Acts 2:42). St. Luke reminds us that the first of Jesus' followers still observed the cycle of Scripture readings in synagogues as a regular part of their worship (Acts 13:14ff). As well, when Christians gathered within the homes of the apostles, the Scriptures were read and preached about at length (Acts 20:9). Whether Greek or Jew, Christians read widely from the Pentateuch, the Law, and the Prophets and paired these with the Gospels and the letters of the apostles as a regular preparation for the celebration of the Eucharist (Justin Martyr, 1 Apol. 67).

SECOND VATICAN COUNCIL

In line with this same ancient tradition, the Second Vatican Council recognized that "Sacred Scripture is of the greatest importance in the celebration of the liturgy. For it is from it that lessons are read and explained in the homily, and psalms are sung. It is from the Scriptures that the prayers, collects, and hymns draw their inspiration and their force, and that actions and signs derive their meaning" (*Constitution on the Liturgy* [*Sacrosanctum concilium*, SC], no. 24). Further, the council declared that the reform of the liturgy should promote an appreciation for the Scriptures by providing the faithful with "more ample, more varied and more suitable" readings at every Mass (SC, no. 35).

This was to be done by opening up treasures of the Bible "more lavishly so that richer fare may be provided for the faithful at the table of God's word. In this way, a more representative part of the Sacred Scriptures will be read to the people in the course of a prescribed number of years" (SC, no. 51).

In response to the council's directives, a revised *Lectionary* was prepared by the Consilium for the Implementation of the Constitution on the Sacred Liturgy under the title *Ordo Lectionum Missae*, approved by Pope Paul VI in the Apostolic Constitution *Missale Romanum* (April 3, 1969) and published by a letter from Benno Cardinal Gut, prefect of the Sacred Congregation for Divine Worship on Pentecost Sunday (May 25, 1969). The letter of publication directed episcopal conferences to prepare vernacular editions of the *Ordo Lectionum Missae* in accordance with the Consilium's 1969 instruction on vernacular translations.

The National Conference of Catholic Bishops (NCCB) published such an edition and decreed its mandatory use in the dioceses of the United States of America beginning with the First Sunday of Advent, November 29, 1971. The biblical text used for this edition was that of the *New American Bible*, a translation first commissioned by the Bishops' Committee for the Confraternity of Christian Doctrine in 1944. For the next two decades, some fifty scholars of the Catholic Biblical Association labored to produce a translation of the Bible from its original languages and the oldest extant texts. Over the first two decades of its use in the liturgy and in private devotion, the 1970 edition of the *New American Bible* has provided immeasurable spiritual benefit.

SECOND EDITION OF THE *ORDO LECTIONUM MISSAE*

In 1981, the Congregation for Divine Worship and the Discipline of the Sacraments issued a second typical edition of the *Ordo Lectionum Missae (editio typica altera)*. This edition was approved by Pope John Paul II and published by a decree from James Cardinal Knox, Prefect of the Congregation, on January 21, 1981.

SECOND EDITION OF THE *LECTIONARY FOR MASS FOR USE IN THE DIOCESES OF THE UNITED STATES OF AMERICA*

The second edition of the *Lectionary for Mass for Use in the Dioceses of the United States of America* was approved by the NCCB on June 20, 1992 and confirmed by the Congregation for Divine Worship and the Discipline of the Sacraments on October 6, 1997.

NEW FEATURES OF THE SECOND EDITION OF THE *ORDO LECTIONUM MISSAE*

The Introduction to the second edition of the *Lectionary for Mass*, which is contained in this edition of the Liturgy Documentary Series, has been considerably expanded. It provides an extended theological introduction to the proclamation of the word of God in the life of the Church and the liturgy. Concrete assistance is then provided for the use of the *Lectionary for Mass*, including a description of the roles appropriate to the liturgy of the word. A final section of the Introduction then describes the structure of the Order of Readings in the second typical edition of the *Lectionary*.

While this volume of the Liturgy Documentary Series is devoted primarily to the Introduction to the *Lectionary*, other elements are also unique to this second typical edition.

Because the first edition of the *Lectionary for Mass* was issued at an early stage in the reform of the liturgical books, the revision of the greater portion of the Roman Ritual and other rites had not yet been completed. Lectionaries developed for those rites which could be celebrated within Mass were not, therefore, incorporated into the first edition of the *Lectionary for Mass*. However, such lectionaries were incorporated into the new edition of the *Lectionary for Mass*.

The 1975 *editio typica altera* of the *Missale Romanum* contained several additional prayer sets for Masses for Various Needs and Occasions. Additional readings were provided in the revised *Lectionary for Mass*, including the following: for the conferral of all sacraments of initiation; for the admission of candidates to the diaconate and the priesthood; for the institution of lectors and acolytes; for the anointing of the sick and dying; for the dedication or blessing of a church or an altar; for the unity of Christians; for the evangelization of peoples; for those in captivity or those who hold others captive. A number of new Masses, such as a votive Mass for the angels, have also been added.

Several major celebrations in the church year were provided with only a single set of readings in the 1970 *Lectionary*. In order that "a more lavish table of the word of God be spread before the faithful" (Cardinal Benno Gut, Decree Promulgating the *Lectionary for Mass*, First Typical Edition, 1969), A, B, and C cycles were provided for celebrations of the Holy Family, the Baptism of the Lord, the Ascension, and Pentecost.

CONCLUSION

The effort to produce a translation of the revised *Lectionary for Mass* has been a nearly ten-year project, involving the combined talents of scholars, bishops, expert consultors, and staff members of both the NCCB Secretariat for the Liturgy and the Congregation for Divine Worship. The greatly expanded choices for celebrating the word of God, which can now be realized in the daily life of the Church, are the result of this important collaborative work. With the publication of the revised *Lectionary for Mass*, a major liturgical book envisioned by the council will now be fully available to support the Church at prayer in the modern world.

Reverend James P. Moroney
Executive Director
NCCB Secretariat for the Liturgy

SACRED CONGREGATION FOR DIVINE WORSHIP

Prot. 106/69

DECREE

The Order of Readings from the Sacred Scriptures to be used at Mass was prepared by the Consilium for the Implementation of the Constitution on the Sacred Liturgy in accordance with the requirement of the Constitution that a more lavish table of the word of God be spread before the faithful, that the treasures of the Bible be opened up more widely, and that the more important part of the Holy Scriptures be read to the people over a prescribed number of years (art. 51). The Supreme Pontiff Paul VI approved it by the Apostolic Constitution *Missale Romanum*, on April 3, 1969.

Accordingly, this Sacred Congregation for Divine Worship, by special mandate of the Supreme Pontiff, promulgates this same Order of Readings for Mass, establishing that it enter into force on November 30, the First Sunday of Advent, in the year 1969. However, in the coming liturgical year series B will be used for the Sunday readings and series II for the first reading on weekdays of Ordinary Time.

Since in the present Order of Readings only the references are given for the individual readings, the Episcopal Conferences will have complete texts prepared in the vernacular languages, observing the norms laid down in the Instruction on vernacular translations issued by the Consilium for the Implementation of the Constitution on the Sacred Liturgy on January 25, 1969. The vernacular texts may either be taken from translations of the Sacred Scriptures already lawfully approved for particular regions, and confirmed by the Apostolic See, or, newly translated, in which case they should be submitted for confirmation to this Sacred Congregation.

All things to the contrary notwithstanding.

From the offices of the Sacred Congregation for Divine Worship, May 25, 1969, Pentecost Sunday.

✝ Benno Cardinal Gut
Prefect

✝ A. Bugnini
Secretary

1

SACRED CONGREGATION FOR THE SACRAMENTS AND DIVINE WORSHIP

Prot. CD 240/81

DECREE

REGARDING THE SECOND TYPICAL EDITION

The Order of Readings for Mass, first published in *editio typica* in 1969, was promulgated on May 25 of that year by special mandate of the Supreme Pontiff Paul VI, in accordance with the requirement of the Constitution on the Sacred Liturgy, in order to provide Bishops' Conferences with the references for the individual biblical readings at Mass with a view to the preparation of lectionaries in the vernacular languages in the different regions.

In that edition were lacking the biblical references of readings for celebration of the sacraments and other rites that have been published since May 1969. Moreover, following the issuing of the Neo-Vulgate edition of the Sacred Scriptures, it was laid down by the Apostolic Constitution *Scripturarum thesaurus* of April 25, 1979 that thereafter the text of the Neo-Vulgate must be adopted as the typical edition for liturgical use. Since the first *editio typica* is no longer available, it seemed opportune to prepare a second edition, having the following features with regard to the previous one:

1. The text of the Introduction has been expanded.
2. In compliance with the Apostolic Constitution *Scripturarum thesaurus*, the Neo-Vulgate edition of the Sacred Scriptures has been used in indicating the biblical references.
3. There have been incorporated all the biblical references to be found in the lectionaries for the celebration of sacraments and sacramentals that have been published since the first edition of the Order of Readings for Mass.
4. The biblical references have also been added for readings for certain Masses "for various needs" and for readings in other Masses which were inserted into the Roman Missal for the first time in its second edition of 1975.

2

5.   As regards the celebrations of the Holy Family, the Baptism of the Lord, the Ascension, and Pentecost, references have been added for optional readings in such a way that biblical texts arranged for cycles A, B, and C in the Lectionary for Sundays and feasts are completed.

The Supreme Pontiff John Paul II has by his authority approved this second edition of the Order of Readings for Mass, and the Sacred Congregation for the Sacraments and Divine Worship now promulgates it and declares it to be the *editio typica.*

The Conferences of Bishops are to see to it that future vernacular editions incorporate the changes contained in this second edition.

The Episcopal Conferences will introduce the changes found in this second edition into the editions to be prepared in the vernacular.

All things to the contrary notwithstanding.

From the offices of the Sacred Congregation for the Sacraments and Divine Worship, January 21, 1981.

✝ James R. Cardinal Knox
Prefect

✝ Virgilio Noè
Associate Secretary

CONGREGATION FOR DIVINE WORSHIP AND THE DISCIPLINE OF THE SACRAMENTS

Prot. 1667/97/L

DECREE

In response to the request of His Excellency Anthony M. Pilla, Bishop of Cleveland, President of the Conference of Bishops of the United States of America, made in a letter dated August 11, 1997, and in virtue of faculties granted to this Congregation by Pope John Paul II, we gladly confirm the first volume of the Mass Lectionary drawn up in English with the title *Lectionary for Mass for Use in the Dioceses of the United States of America*, and annexed to this decree.

In printed editions of the text there should be inserted in its entirety this Decree by which the Apostolic See accords the requested confirmation of the sole translation to be used in the celebration of Holy Mass in all the dioceses of the United States of America. Moreover, two copies of the printed text should be forwarded to this Congregation.

All things to the contrary notwithstanding.

From the offices of the Congregation for Divine Worship and the Discipline of the Sacraments, October 6, 1997.

✝ Jorge Medina Estévez
Pro-Prefect

✝ Geraldo M. Agnelo
Archbishop Secretary

NATIONAL CONFERENCE OF CATHOLIC BISHOPS
UNITED STATES OF AMERICA

DECREE

In accord with the norms established by decree of the Sacred Congregation of Rites in *Cum, nostra ætate* (January 27, 1966), this edition of the *Lectionary for Mass, Volume I: Sundays, Solemnities, and Feasts of the Lord* is declared to be the vernacular typical edition of the *Ordo Lectionum Missae, editio typica altera* in the dioceses of the United States of America, and is published by authority of the National Conference of Catholic Bishops.

The first volume of the *Lectionary for Mass* was canonically approved for use by the National Conference of Catholic Bishops on June 20, 1992 and was subsequently confirmed by the Apostolic See by decree of the Congregation for Divine Worship and the Discipline of the Sacraments on October 6, 1997 (Prot. 1667/97/L).

On the First Sunday of Advent, November 29, 1998, the first volume of the *Lectionary for Mass* may be used in the liturgy. Upon promulgation of the second volume of the *Lectionary for Mass* a date for mandatory use will be established.

Given at the General Secretariat of the National Conference of Catholic Bishops, Washington D.C. on June 19, 1998, the Solemnity of the Sacred Heart of Jesus.

Most Reverend Anthony M. Pilla
Bishop of Cleveland
President
National Conference of Catholic
Bishops

Reverend Monsignor Dennis M. Schnurr
General Secretary

LECTIONARY FOR MASS

INTRODUCTION

Preamble

CHAPTER I
GENERAL PRINCIPLES FOR THE LITURGICAL
CELEBRATION OF THE WORD OF GOD

1. CERTAIN PRELIMINARIES

a) The Importance of the Word of God
in Liturgical Celebration

1.   The Second Vatican Council,[1] the magisterium of the Popes,[2] and various documents promulgated after the Council by the organisms of the Holy See[3] have already had many excellent things to say about the importance of the word of God and about reestablishing the use of Sacred Scripture in every celebration of the Liturgy. The Introduction to the 1969 edition of the Order of Readings for Mass has clearly stated and briefly explained some of the more important principles.[4]

On the occasion of this new edition of the Order of Readings for Mass, requests have come from many quarters for a more detailed exposition of the same principles. Hence, this expanded and more suitable arrangement of the Introduction first gives a general statement on the essential bond between the word of God and the liturgical celebration,[5] then deals in greater detail with the word of God in the celebration of Mass, and, finally, explains the precise structure of the Order of Readings for Mass.

b) Terms Used to Refer to the Word of God

2.   For the sake of clear and precise language on this topic, a definition of terms might well be expected as a prerequisite. Nevertheless this Introduction will simply use the same terms employed in conciliar and postconciliar documents. Furthermore it will use "Sacred Scripture" and "word of God" interchangeably throughout when referring to the books written under the inspiration of the Holy Spirit, thus avoiding any confusion of language or meaning.[6]

9

c) The Significance of the Word of God in the Liturgy

3.   The many riches contained in the one word of God are admirably brought out in the different kinds of liturgical celebration and in the different gatherings of the faithful who take part in those celebrations. This takes place as the unfolding mystery of Christ is recalled during the course of the liturgical year, as the Church's sacraments and sacramentals are celebrated, or as the faithful respond individually to the Holy Spirit working within them.[7] For them the liturgical celebration, founded primarily on the word of God and sustained by it, becomes a new event and enriches the word itself with new meaning and power. Thus in the Liturgy the Church faithfully adheres to the way Christ himself read and explained the Sacred Scriptures, beginning with the "today" of his coming forward in the synagogue and urging all to search the Scriptures.[8]

2. LITURGICAL CELEBRATION OF THE WORD OF GOD

a) The Proper Character of the Word of God in the Liturgical Celebration

4.   In the celebration of the liturgy the word of God is not announced in only one way[9] nor does it always stir the hearts of the hearers with the same efficacy. Always, however, Christ is present in his word[10]; as he carries out the mystery of salvation, he sanctifies humanity and offers the Father perfect worship.[11]

Moreover, the word of God unceasingly calls to mind and extends the economy of salvation, which achieves its fullest expression in the Liturgy. The liturgical celebration becomes therefore the continuing, complete, and effective presentation of God's word.

The word of God constantly proclaimed in the Liturgy is always, then, a living and effective word[12] through the power of the Holy Spirit. It expresses the Father's love that never fails in its effectiveness toward us.

b) The Word of God in the Economy of Salvation

5.   When in celebrating the Liturgy the Church proclaims both the Old and New Testament, it is proclaiming one and the same mystery of Christ.

The New Testament lies hidden in the Old; the Old Testament comes fully to light in the New.[13] Christ himself is the center and fullness of the whole of Scripture, just as he is of all liturgical celebration.[14] Thus the Scriptures are the living waters from which all who seek life and salvation must drink.

The more profound our understanding of the celebration of the liturgy, the higher our appreciation of the importance of God's word. Whatever we say of the one, we can in turn say of the other, because each recalls the mystery of Christ and each in its own way causes the mystery to be carried forward.

c) The Word of God in the Liturgical Participation of the Faithful

6. In celebrating the Liturgy, the Church faithfully echoes the "Amen" that Christ, the mediator between God and men and women, uttered once for all as he shed his blood to seal God's new covenant in the Holy Spirit.[15]

When God communicates his word, he expects a response, one that is of listening and adoring "in Spirit and in truth" (Jn 4:23). The Holy Spirit makes that response effective, so that what is heard in the celebration of the Liturgy may be carried out in a way of life: "Be doers of the word and not hearers only" (Jas 1:22).

The liturgical celebration and the participation of the faithful receive outward expression in actions, gestures, and words. These derive their full meaning not simply from their origin in human experience but from the word of God and the economy of salvation, to which they refer. Accordingly, the participation of the faithful in the Liturgy increases to the degree that, as they listen to the word of God proclaimed in the Liturgy, they strive harder to commit themselves to the Word of God incarnate in Christ. Thus, they endeavor to conform their way of life to what they celebrate in the Liturgy, and then in turn to bring to the celebration of the Liturgy all that they do in life.[16]

3. THE WORD OF GOD IN THE LIFE OF THE PEOPLE OF THE COVENANT

a) The Word of God in the Life of the Church

7. In the hearing of God's word the Church is built up and grows, and in the signs of the liturgical celebration, God's wonderful, past works in the history of salvation are presented anew as mysterious realities. God in turn makes use of the congregation of the faithful that celebrates the Liturgy in order that his word may speed on and be glorified and that his name be exalted among the nations.[17]

Whenever, therefore, the Church, gathered by the Holy Spirit for liturgical celebration,[18] announces and proclaims the word of God, she is aware of being a new people in whom the covenant made in the past is perfected and fulfilled. Baptism and confirmation in the Spirit have made all Christ's faithful into messengers of God's word because of the grace of hearing they have received. They must therefore be the bearers of the same word in the Church and in the world, at least by the witness of their lives.

The word of God proclaimed in the celebration of God's mysteries does not only address present conditions but looks back to past events and forward to what is yet to come. Thus God's word shows us what we should hope for with such a longing that in this changing world our hearts will be set on the place where our true joys lie.[19]

b) The Church's Explanation of the Word of God

8. By Christ's own will there is a marvelous diversity of members in the new people of God, and each has different duties and responsibilities with respect to the word of God. Accordingly, the faithful listen to God's word and meditate on it, but only those who have the office of teaching by virtue of sacred ordination or who have been entrusted with exercising that ministry expound the word of God.

This is how in doctrine, life, and worship the Church keeps alive and passes on to every generation all that she is, all that she believes. Thus with the passage of the centuries, the Church is ever to advance toward the fullness of divine truth until God's word is wholly accomplished in her.[20]

c) The Connection Between the Word of God Proclaimed and the Working of the Holy Spirit

9. The working of the Holy Spirit is needed if the word of God is to make what we hear outwardly have its effect inwardly. Because of the Holy Spirit's inspiration and support, the word of God becomes the foundation of the liturgical celebration and the rule and support of all our life.

The working of the Holy Spirit precedes, accompanies, and brings to completion the whole celebration of the Liturgy. But the Spirit also brings home[21] to each person individually everything that in the proclamation of the word of God is spoken for the good of the whole gathering of the faithful. In strengthening the unity of all, the Holy Spirit at the same time fosters a diversity of gifts and furthers their multiform operation.

d) The Essential Bond Between the Word of God and the Mystery of the Eucharist

10. The Church has honored the word of God and the Eucharistic mystery with the same reverence, although not with the same worship, and has always and everywhere insisted upon and sanctioned such honor. Moved by the example of its Founder, the Church has never ceased to celebrate his paschal mystery by coming together to read "what referred to him in all the Scriptures" (Lk 24:27) and to carry out the work of salvation through the celebration of the memorial of the Lord and through the sacraments. "The preaching of the word is necessary for the ministry of the sacraments, for these are sacraments of faith, which is born and nourished from the word."[22]

The Church is nourished spiritually at the twofold table of God's word and of the Eucharist:[23] from the one it grows in wisdom and from the other in holiness. In the word of God the divine covenant is announced; in the Eucharist the new and everlasting covenant is renewed. On the one hand the history of salvation is brought to mind by means of human sounds; on the other it is made manifest in the sacramental signs of the Liturgy.

It can never be forgotten, therefore, that the divine word read and proclaimed by the Church in the Liturgy has as its one purpose the sacrifice of the New Covenant and the banquet of grace, that is, the Eucharist. The celebration of Mass in which the word is heard and the Eucharist is offered and received forms but one single act of divine worship.[24] That act offers the sacrifice of praise to God and makes available to God's creatures the fullness of redemption.

First Part: The Word of God in the Celebration of Mass

CHAPTER II
THE CELEBRATION OF THE LITURGY
OF THE WORD AT MASS

1. THE ELEMENTS OF THE LITURGY
OF THE WORD AND THEIR RITES

11. "Readings from Sacred Scripture and the chants between the readings form the main part of the liturgy of the word. The homily, the profession of faith, and the universal prayer or prayer of the faithful carry it forward and conclude it."[25]

a) The Biblical Readings

12. In the celebration of Mass, the biblical readings with their accompanying chants from the Sacred Scriptures may not be omitted, shortened, or, worse still, replaced by nonbiblical readings.[26] For it is out of the word of God handed down in writing that even now "God speaks to his people,"[27] and it is from the continued use of Sacred Scripture that the people of God, docile to the Holy Spirit under the light of faith, is enabled to bear witness to Christ before the world by its manner of life.

13. The reading of the Gospel is the high point of the liturgy of the word. For this the other readings, in their established sequence from the Old to the New Testament, prepare the assembly.

14. A speaking style on the part of the readers that is audible, clear, and intelligent is the first means of transmitting the word of God properly to the congregation. The readings, taken from the approved editions,[28] may be sung in a way suited to different languages. This singing, however, must serve to bring out the sense of the words, not obscure them. On occasions when the readings are in Latin, the manner given in the *Ordo cantus Missae* is to be maintained.[29]

15. There may be concise introductions before the readings, especially the first. The style proper to such comments must be respected, that is, they must be simple, faithful to the text, brief, well prepared, and properly varied to suit the text they introduce.[30]

14

16. In a Mass with the people, the readings are always to be proclaimed at the ambo.[31]

17. Of all the rites connected with the liturgy of the word, the reverence due to the Gospel reading must receive special attention.[32] Where there is an Evangeliary or Book of Gospels that has been carried in by the deacon or reader during the entry procession,[33] it is most fitting that the deacon or a priest, when there is no deacon, take the book from the altar[34] and carry it to the ambo. He is preceded by servers with candles and incense or other symbols of reverence that may be customary. As the faithful stand and acclaim the Lord, they show honor to the Book of Gospels. The deacon who is to read the Gospel, bowing in front of the one presiding, asks and receives the blessing. When no deacon is present, the priest, bowing before the altar, prays inaudibly, *Almighty God, cleanse my heart. . . .*[35]

At the ambo the one who proclaims the Gospel greets the people, who are standing, and announces the reading as he makes the sign of the cross on forehead, mouth, and breast. If incense is used, he next incenses the book, then reads the Gospel. When finished, he kisses the book, saying the appointed words inaudibly.

Even if the Gospel itself is not sung, it is appropriate for the greeting *The Lord be with you*, and *A reading from the holy Gospel according to . . .*, and at the end *The Gospel of the Lord* to be sung, in order that the congregation may also sing its acclamations. This is a way both of bringing out the importance of the Gospel reading and of stirring up the faith of those who hear it.

18. At the conclusion of the other readings, *The word of the Lord* may be sung, even by someone other than the reader; all respond with the acclamation. In this way the assembled congregation pays reverence to the word of God it has listened to in faith and gratitude.

b) The Responsorial Psalm

19. The responsorial psalm, also called the gradual, has great liturgical and pastoral significance because it is an "integral part of the liturgy of the word."[36] Accordingly, the faithful must be continually instructed on the way to perceive the word of God speaking in the psalms and to turn these psalms into the prayer of the Church. This, of course, "will be achieved more readily if a deeper understanding of the psalms, according to the meaning with which they are sung in the sacred Liturgy, is more diligently promoted among the clergy and communicated to all the faithful by means of appropriate catechesis."[37]

Brief remarks about the choice of the psalm and response as well as their correspondence to the readings may be helpful.

20. As a rule the responsorial psalm should be sung. There are two established ways of singing the psalm after the first reading: responsorially and directly. In responsorial singing, which, as far as possible, is to be given preference, the psalmist, or cantor of the psalm, sings the psalm verse and the whole congregation joins in by singing the response. In direct singing of the psalm, there is no intervening response by the community; either the psalmist, or cantor of the psalm, sings the psalm alone as the community listens or else all sing it together.

21. The singing of the psalm, or even of the response alone, is a great help toward understanding and meditating on the psalm's spiritual meaning.

To foster the congregation's singing, every means available in each individual culture is to be employed. In particular, use is to be made of all the relevant options provided in the Order of Readings for Mass[38] regarding responses corresponding to the different liturgical seasons.

22. When not sung, the psalm after the reading is to be recited in a manner conducive to meditation on the word of God.[39]

The responsorial psalm is sung or recited by the psalmist or cantor at the ambo.[40]

c) The Acclamation Before the Reading of the Gospel

23. The *Alleluia* or, as the liturgical season requires, the verse before the Gospel, is also a "rite or act standing by itself."[41] It serves as the greeting of welcome of the assembled faithful to the Lord who is about to speak to them and as an expression of their faith through song.

The *Alleluia* or the verse before the Gospel must be sung and during it all stand. It is not to be sung only by the cantor who intones it or by the choir, but by the whole of the people together.[42]

d) The Homily

24. Through the course of the liturgical year, the homily sets forth the mysteries of faith and the standards of the Christian life on the basis of the sacred text. Beginning with the Constitution on the Liturgy, the homily as part of the liturgy of the word[43] has been repeatedly and strongly recommended and in some cases it is obligatory. As a rule it is to be given by the one presiding.[44] The purpose of the homily at Mass is that the spoken word of God and the liturgy of the Eucharist may together become "a proclamation of God's wonderful works in the history of salvation, the mystery of Christ."[45] Through the readings and homily, Christ's paschal mystery is proclaimed; through the sacrifice of the Mass, it becomes present.[46] Moreover Christ himself is always present and active in the preaching of his Church.[47]

Whether the homily explains the text of the Sacred Scriptures proclaimed in the readings or some other text of the Liturgy,[48] it must always lead the community of the faithful to celebrate the Eucharist actively, "so that they may hold fast in their lives to what they have grasped by faith."[49] From this living explanation, the word of God proclaimed in the readings and the Church's celebration of the day's Liturgy will have greater impact. But this demands that the homily be truly the fruit of meditation, carefully prepared, neither too long nor too short, and suited to all those present, even children and the uneducated.[50]

At a concelebration, the celebrant or one of the concelebrants as a rule gives the homily.[51]

25. On the prescribed days, that is, Sundays and holy days of obligation, there must be a homily in all Masses celebrated with a congregation, even Masses on the preceding evening; the homily may not be omitted without a serious reason.[52] There is also to be a homily in Masses with children and with special groups.[53]

A homily is strongly recommended on the weekdays of Advent, Lent, and the Easter season for the sake of the faithful who regularly take part in the celebration of Mass; also on other feasts and occasions when a large congregation is present.[54]

26. The priest celebrant gives the homily, standing either at the chair or at the ambo.[55]

27. Any necessary announcements are to be kept completely separate from the homily; they must take place following the prayer after Communion.[56]

e) Silence

28. The liturgy of the word must be celebrated in a way that fosters meditation; clearly, any sort of haste that hinders recollection must be avoided. The dialogue between God and his people taking place through the Holy Spirit demands short intervals of silence, suited to the assembled congregation, as an opportunity to take the word of God to heart and to prepare a response to it in prayer.

Proper times for silence during the liturgy of the word are, for example, before this liturgy begins, after the first and the second reading, after the homily.[57]

f) The Profession of Faith

29. The symbol, creed, or profession of faith, said when the rubrics require, has as its purpose in the celebration of Mass that the assembled congregation may respond and give assent to the word of God heard in the readings and through the homily, and that before beginning to celebrate in the Eucharist the mystery of faith it may call to mind the rule of faith in a formulary approved by the Church.[58]

g) The Universal Prayer or Prayer of the Faithful

30.　In the light of God's word and in a sense in response to it, the congregation of the faithful prays in the universal prayer as a rule for the needs of the universal Church and the local community, for the salvation of the world and those oppressed by any burden, and for special categories of people.

The celebrant introduces the prayer; a deacon, another minister, or some of the faithful may propose intentions that are short and phrased with a measure of freedom. In these petitions "the people, exercising its priestly function, makes intercession for all men and women,"[59] with the result that, as the liturgy of the word has its full effects in the faithful, they are better prepared to proceed to the liturgy of the Eucharist.

31.　For the prayer of the faithful, the celebrant presides at the chair and the intentions are announced at the ambo.[60]

The assembled congregation takes part in the prayer of the faithful while standing and by saying or singing a common response after each intention or by silent prayer.[61]

2. AIDS TO THE PROPER CELEBRATION OF THE LITURGY OF THE WORD

a) The Place for the Proclamation of the Word of God

32.　There must be a place in the church that is somewhat elevated, fixed, and of a suitable design and nobility. It should reflect the dignity of God's word and be a clear reminder to the people that in the Mass the table of God's word and of Christ's body is placed before them.[62] The place for the readings must also truly help the people's listening and attention during the liturgy of the word. Great pains must therefore be taken, in keeping with the design of each church, over the harmonious and close relationship of the ambo with the altar.

33.　Either permanently or at least on occasions of greater solemnity, the ambo should be decorated simply and in keeping with its design.

Since the ambo is the place from which the word of God is proclaimed by the ministers, it must of its nature be reserved for the readings, the responsorial psalm, and the Easter Proclamation (the *Exsultet*). The ambo may rightly be used for the homily and the prayer of the faithful, however, because of their close connection with the entire liturgy of the word. It is better for the commentator, cantor, or director of singing, for example, not to use the ambo.[63]

34. In order that the ambo may properly serve its liturgical purpose, it is to be rather large, since on occasion several ministers must use it at the same time. Provision must also be made for the readers to have enough light to read the text and, as required, to have modern sound equipment enabling the faithful to hear them without difficulty.

b) The Books for Proclamation of the Word of God in the Liturgy

35. Along with the ministers, the actions, the allocated places, and other elements, the books containing the readings of the word of God remind the hearers of the presence of God speaking to his people. Since in liturgical celebrations the books too serve as signs and symbols of the higher realities, care must be taken to ensure that they truly are worthy, dignified, and beautiful.[64]

36. The proclamation of the Gospel always stands as the high point of the liturgy of the word. Thus the liturgical tradition of both West and East has consistently made a certain distinction between the books for the readings. The Book of Gospels was always fabricated and decorated with the utmost care and shown greater respect than any of the other books of readings. In our times also, then, it is very desirable that cathedrals and at least the larger, more populous parishes and the churches with a larger attendance possess a beautifully designed Book of Gospels, separate from any other book of readings. For good reason, it is the Book of Gospels that is presented to a deacon at his ordination and that at an ordination to the episcopate is laid upon the head of the bishop-elect and held there.[65]

37. Because of the dignity of the word of God, the books of readings used in the celebration are not to be replaced by other pastoral aids, for example, by leaflets printed for the preparation of the readings by the faithful or for their personal meditation.

CHAPTER III
OFFICES AND MINISTRIES
IN THE CELEBRATION OF THE LITURGY
OF THE WORD WITHIN MASS

1. THE FUNCTION OF THE PRESIDENT
AT THE LITURGY OF THE WORD

38.   The one presiding at the liturgy of the word communicates the spiritual nourishment it contains to those present, especially in the homily. Even if he too is a listener to the word of God proclaimed by others, the duty of proclaiming it has been entrusted above all to him. Personally or through others he sees to it that the word of God is properly proclaimed. He then as a rule reserves to himself the tasks of composing comments to help the people listen more attentively and of preaching a homily that fosters in them a richer understanding of the word of God.

39.   The first requirement for one who is to preside over the celebration is a thorough knowledge of the structure of the Order of Readings, so that he will know how to work a fruitful effect in the hearts of the faithful. Through study and prayer he must also develop a full understanding of the coordination and connection of the various texts in the liturgy of the word, so that the Order of Readings will become the source of a sound understanding of the mystery of Christ and his saving work.

40.   The one presiding is to make ready use of the various options provided in the Lectionary regarding readings, responses, responsorial psalms, and Gospel acclamations;[66] but he is to do so in harmony[67] with all concerned and after listening to the opinions of the faithful in what concerns them.[68]

41.   The one presiding exercises his proper office and the ministry of the word of God also as he preaches the homily.[69] In this way, he leads his brothers and sisters to an affective knowledge of Scripture. He opens their minds to thanksgiving for the wonderful works of God. He strengthens the faith of those present in the word that in the celebration becomes sacrament through the Holy Spirit. Finally, he prepares them for a fruitful reception of Communion and invites them to take upon themselves the demands of the Christian life.

42. The president is responsible for preparing the faithful for the liturgy of the word on occasion by means of introductions before the readings.[70] These comments can help the assembled congregation toward a better hearing of the word of God, because they stir up an attitude of faith and good will. He may also carry out this responsibility through others, a deacon, for example, or a commentator.[71]

43. As he directs the prayer of the faithful and through their introduction and conclusion connects them, if possible, with the day's readings and the homily, the president leads the faithful toward the liturgy of the Eucharist.[72]

2. THE ROLE OF THE FAITHFUL IN THE LITURGY OF THE WORD

44. Christ's word gathers the people of God as one and increases and sustains them. "This applies above all to the liturgy of the word in the celebration of Mass, where there are inseparably united the proclamation of the death of the Lord, the response of the people listening, and the very offering through which Christ has confirmed the New Covenant in his Blood, and in which the people share by their intentions and by reception of the sacrament."[73] For "not only when things are read 'that were written for our instruction' (Rom 15:4), but also when the Church prays or sings or acts, the faith of those taking part is nourished and their minds are raised to God, so that they may offer him rightful worship and receive his grace more abundantly."[74]

45. In the liturgy of the word, the congregation of Christ's faithful even today receives from God the word of his covenant through the faith that comes by hearing, and must respond to that word in faith, so that they may become more and more truly the people of the New Covenant.

The people of God have a spiritual right to receive abundantly from the treasury of God's word. Its riches are presented to them through use of the Order of Readings, the homily, and pastoral efforts.

For their part, the faithful at the celebration of Mass are to listen to the word of God with an inward and outward reverence that will bring them continuous growth in the spiritual life and draw them more deeply into the mystery which is celebrated.[75]

46. As a help toward celebrating the memorial of the Lord with eager devotion, the faithful should be keenly aware of the one presence of Christ in both the word of God—it is he himself "who speaks when the Sacred Scriptures are read in the Church"—and "above all under the Eucharistic species."[76]

47. To be received and integrated into the life of Christ's faithful, the word of God demands a living faith.[77] Hearing the word of God unceasingly proclaimed arouses that faith.

The Sacred Scriptures, above all in their liturgical proclamation, are the source of life and strength. As the Apostle Paul attests, the Gospel is the saving power of God for everyone who believes.[78] Love of the Scriptures is therefore a force reinvigorating and renewing the entire people of God.[79] All the faithful without exception must therefore always be ready to listen gladly to God's word.[80] When this word is proclaimed in the Church and put into living practice, it enlightens the faithful through the working of the Holy Spirit and draws them into the entire mystery of the Lord as a reality to be lived.[81] The word of God reverently received moves the heart and its desires toward conversion and toward a life resplendent with both individual and community faith,[82] since God's word is the food of Christian life and the source of the prayer of the whole Church.[83]

48. The intimate connection between the liturgy of the word and the liturgy of the Eucharist in the Mass should prompt the faithful to be present right from the beginning of the celebration,[84] to take part attentively, and to prepare themselves insofar as possible to hear the word, especially by learning beforehand more about Sacred Scripture. That same connection should also awaken in them a desire for a liturgical understanding of the texts read and a readiness to respond through singing.[85]

When they hear the word of God and reflect deeply on it, Christ's faithful are enabled to respond to it actively with full faith, hope, and charity through prayer and self-giving, and not only during Mass but in their entire Christian life.

3. MINISTRIES IN THE LITURGY OF THE WORD

49. Liturgical tradition assigns responsibility for the biblical readings in the celebration of Mass to ministers: to readers and the deacon. But when there is no deacon or no other priest present, the priest celebrant is to read the Gospel[86] and when there is no reader present, all the readings.[87]

50. It pertains to the deacon in the liturgy of the word at Mass to proclaim the Gospel, sometimes to give the homily, as occasion suggests, and to propose to the people the intentions of the prayer of the faithful.[88]

51. "The reader has his own proper function in the Eucharistic celebration and should exercise this even though ministers of a higher rank may be present."[89] The ministry of reader, conferred through a liturgical rite, must be held in respect. When there are instituted readers available, they are to carry out their office at least on Sundays and festive days, especially at the principal Mass of the day. These readers may also be given responsibility for assisting in the arrangement of the liturgy of the word, and, to the extent necessary, of seeing to the preparation of others of the faithful who may be appointed on a given occasion to read at Mass.[90]

52. The liturgical assembly truly requires readers, even those not instituted. Proper measures must therefore be taken to ensure that there are certain suitable laypeople who have been trained to carry out this ministry.[91] Whenever there is more than one reading, it is better to assign the readings to different readers, if available.

53. In Masses without a deacon, the function of announcing the intentions for the prayer of the faithful is to be assigned to the cantor, particularly when they are to be sung, to a reader, or to someone else.[92]

54. During the celebration of Mass with a congregation, a second priest, a deacon, and an instituted reader must wear the distinctive vestment of their office when they go up to the ambo to read the word of God. Those who carry out the ministry of reader just for the occasion or even regularly but without institution may go to the ambo in ordinary attire, but this should be in keeping with the customs of the different regions.

55. "It is necessary that those who exercise the ministry of reader, even if they have not received institution, be truly suited and carefully prepared, so that the faithful may develop a warm and living love for Sacred Scripture from listening to the sacred readings."[93]

Their preparation must above all be spiritual, but what may be called a technical preparation is also needed. The spiritual preparation presupposes at least a biblical and liturgical formation. The purpose of their biblical formation is to give readers the ability to understand the readings in context and to perceive by the light of faith the central point of the revealed message. The liturgical formation ought to equip the readers to have some grasp of the meaning and structure of the liturgy of the word and of the significance of its connection with the liturgy of the Eucharist. The technical preparation should make the readers more skilled in the art of reading publicly, either with the power of their own voice or with the help of sound equipment.

56. The psalmist, or cantor of the psalm, is responsible for singing, responsorially or directly, the chants between the readings—the psalm or other biblical canticle, the gradual and *Alleluia*, or other chant. The psalmist may, as occasion requires, intone the *Alleluia* and verse.[94]

For carrying out the function of psalmist, it is advantageous to have in each ecclesial community laypeople with the ability to sing and read with correct diction. The points made about the formation of readers apply to cantors as well.

57. The commentator also fulfills a genuine liturgical ministry, which consists in presenting to the congregation of the faithful, from a suitable place, relevant explanations and comments that are clear, of marked sobriety, meticulously prepared, and as a rule written out and approved beforehand by the celebrant.[95]

Second Part: The Structure of the Order of Readings for Mass

CHAPTER IV
THE GENERAL ARRANGEMENT
OF READINGS FOR MASS

1. THE PASTORAL PURPOSE OF THE ORDER OF READINGS FOR MASS

58. On the basis of the intention of the Second Vatican Council, the Order of Readings provided by the Lectionary of the Roman Missal has been composed above all for a pastoral purpose. To achieve this aim, not only the principles underlying this new Order of Readings but also the lists of texts that it provides have been discussed and revised over and over again, with the cooperation of a great many experts in exegetical, liturgical, catechetical, and pastoral studies from all parts of the world. The Order of Readings is the fruit of this combined effort.

The prolonged use of this Order of Readings to proclaim and explain Sacred Scripture in the Eucharistic celebration will, it is hoped, prove to be an effective step toward achieving the objective stated repeatedly by the Second Vatican Council.[96]

59. The decision on revising the Lectionary for Mass was to draw up and edit a single, rich, and full Order of Readings that would be in complete accord with the intent and prescriptions of the Second Vatican Council.[97] At the same time, however, the Order was meant to be of a kind that would meet the requirements and usages of particular Churches and celebrating congregations. For this reason, those responsible for the revision took pains to safeguard the liturgical tradition of the Roman Rite, but valued highly the merits of all the systems of selecting, arranging, and using the biblical readings in other liturgical families and in certain particular Churches. The revisers made use of those elements that experience has confirmed, but with an effort to avoid certain shortcomings found in the preceding form of the tradition.

60. The present Order of Readings for Mass, then, is an arrangement of biblical readings that provides the faithful with a knowledge of the whole of God's word, in a pattern suited to the purpose. Throughout the liturgical year, but above all during the seasons of Easter, Lent, and Advent, the choice and sequence of readings are aimed at giving Christ's faithful an ever-deepening perception of the faith they profess and of the history of salvation.[98] Accordingly, the Order of Readings corresponds to the requirements and interests of the Christian people.

61. The celebration of the Liturgy is not in itself simply a form of catechesis, but it does contain an element of teaching. The Lectionary of the Roman Missal brings this out[99] and therefore deserves to be regarded as a pedagogical resource aiding catechesis.

This is so because the Order of Readings for Mass aptly presents from Sacred Scripture the principal deeds and words belonging to the history of salvation. As its many phases and events are recalled in the liturgy of the word, it will become clear to the faithful that the history of salvation is continued here and now in the representation of Christ's paschal mystery celebrated through the Eucharist.

62. The pastoral advantage of having in the Roman Rite a single Order of Readings for the Lectionary is obvious on other grounds. All the faithful, particularly those who for various reasons do not always take part in Mass with the same assembly, will everywhere be able to hear the same readings on any given day or in any liturgical season and to meditate on the application of these readings to their own concrete circumstances. This is the case even in places that have no priest and where a deacon or someone else deputed by the bishop conducts a celebration of the word of God.[100]

63. Pastors may wish to respond specifically from the word of God to the concerns of their own congregations. Although they must be mindful that they are above all to be heralds of the entire mystery of Christ and of the Gospel, they may rightfully use the options provided in the Order of Readings for Mass. This applies particularly to the celebration of a ritual or votive Mass, a Mass in honor of the Saints, or one of the Masses for various needs and occasions. With due regard for the general norms, special faculties are granted concerning the readings in Masses celebrated for particular groups.[101]

2. THE PRINCIPLES OF COMPOSITION OF THE ORDER OF READINGS FOR MASS

64. To achieve the purpose of the Order of Readings for Mass, the parts have been selected and arranged in such a way as to take into account the sequence of the liturgical seasons and the hermeneutical principles whose understanding and definition has been facilitated by modern biblical research.

It was judged helpful to state here the principles guiding the composition of the Order of Readings for Mass.

a) The Choice of Texts

65. The course of readings in the Proper of Seasons is arranged as follows. Sundays and festive days present the more important biblical passages. In this way the more significant parts of God's revealed word can be read to the assembled faithful within an appropriate period of time. Weekdays present a second series of texts from Sacred Scripture and in a sense these complement the message of salvation explained on festive days. But neither series in these main parts of the Order of Readings—the series for Sundays and festive days and that for weekdays—is dependent on the other. The Order of Readings for Sundays and festive days extends over three years; for weekdays, over two. Thus each runs its course independently of the other.

The sequence of readings in other parts of the Order of Readings is governed by its own rules. This applies to the series of readings for celebrations of the Saints, ritual Masses, Masses for various needs and occasions, votive Masses, or Masses for the dead.

b) The Arrangement of the Readings for Sundays and Festive Days

66. The following are features proper to the readings for Sundays and festive days:

1. Each Mass has three readings: the first from the Old Testament, the second from an Apostle (that is, either from a Letter or from the Book of Revelation, depending on the season), and the third from the Gospels. This arrangement brings out the unity of the Old and New Testaments and of the history of salvation, in which Christ is the central figure, commemorated in his paschal mystery.

2. A more varied and richer reading of Sacred Scripture on Sundays and festive days results from the three-year cycle provided for these days, in that the same texts are read only every fourth year.[102]

3. The principles governing the Order of Reading for Sundays and festive days are called the principles of "harmony" and of "semi-continuous reading." One or the other applies according to the different seasons of the year and the distinctive character of the particular liturgical season.

67. The best instance of harmony between the Old and New Testament readings occurs when it is one that Scripture itself suggests. This is the case when the doctrine and events recounted in texts of the New Testament bear a more or less explicit relationship to the doctrine and events of the Old Testament. The present Order of Readings selects Old Testament texts mainly because of their correlation with New Testament texts read in the same Mass, and particularly with the Gospel text.

Harmony of another kind exists between texts of the readings for each Mass during Advent, Lent, and Easter, the seasons that have a distinctive importance or character.

In contrast, the Sundays in Ordinary Time do not have a distinctive character. Thus the text of both the apostolic and Gospel readings are arranged in order of semicontinuous reading, whereas the Old Testament reading is harmonized with the Gospel.

68. The decision was made not to extend to Sundays the arrangement suited to the liturgical seasons mentioned, that is, not to have an organic harmony of themes devised with a view to facilitating homiletic instruction. Such an arrangement would be in conflict with the genuine conception of liturgical celebration, which is always the celebration of the mystery of Christ and which by its own tradition makes use of the word of God not only at the prompting of logical or extrinsic concerns but spurred by the desire to proclaim the Gospel and to lead those who believe to the fullness of truth.

c) The Arrangement of the Readings for Weekdays

69. The weekday readings have been arranged in the following way:

1. Each Mass has two readings: the first is from the Old Testament or from an Apostle (that is, either from a Letter or from the Book of Revelation), and during the Easter season from the Acts of the Apostles; the second, from the Gospels.

2. The yearly cycle for Lent has its own principles of arrangement, which take into account the baptismal and penitential character of this season.

3. The cycle for the weekdays of Advent, the Christmas season, and the Easter season is also yearly and the readings thus remain the same each year.

4. For the thirty-four weeks of Ordinary Time, the weekday Gospel readings are arranged in a single cycle, repeated each year. But the first reading is arranged in a two-year cycle and is thus read every other year. Year I is used during odd-numbered years; Year II, during even-numbered years.

Like the Order for Sundays and festive days, then, the weekday Order of Readings is governed by similar application of the principles of harmony and of semicontinuous reading, especially in the case of seasons with their own distinctive character.

d) The Readings for Celebrations of the Saints

70. Two series of readings are provided for celebrations of the Saints.

1. The Proper of Saints provides the first series, for solemnities, feasts, or memorials and particularly when there are proper texts for one or other such celebration. Sometimes in the Proper, however, there is a reference to the most appropriate among the texts in the Commons as the one to be given preference.

2. The Commons of Saints provide the second, more extensive group of readings. There are, first, appropriate texts for the different classes of Saints (martyrs, pastors, virgins, etc.), then numerous texts that deal with holiness in general. These may be freely chosen whenever the Commons are indicated as the source for the choice of readings.

71. As to their sequence, all the texts in this part of the Order of Readings appear in the order in which they are to be read at Mass. Thus the Old Testament texts are first, then the texts from the Apostles, followed by the psalms and verses between the readings, and finally the texts from the Gospels. The rationale of this arrangement is that, unless otherwise noted, the celebrant may choose at will from such texts, in view of the pastoral needs of the congregation taking part in the celebration.

e) Readings for Ritual Masses, Masses for Various Needs and Occasions, Votive Masses, and Masses for the Dead

72. For ritual Masses, Masses for various needs and occasions, votive Masses, and Masses for the dead, the texts for the readings are arranged as just described, that is, numerous texts are grouped together in the order of their use, as in the Commons of Saints.

f) The Main Criteria Applied in Choosing and Arranging the Readings

73. In addition to the guiding principles already given for the arrangement of readings in the individual parts of the Order of Readings, others of a more general nature follow.

1) The Reservation of Some Books to Particular Liturgical Seasons

74. In this Order of Readings, some biblical books are set aside for particular liturgical seasons on the basis both of the intrinsic importance of subject matter and of liturgical tradition. For example, the Western (Ambrosian and Hispanic) and Eastern tradition of reading the Acts of the

Apostles during the Easter season is maintained. This usage results in a clear presentation of how the Church's entire life derives its beginning from the paschal mystery. The tradition of both West and East is also retained, namely the reading of the Gospel of John in the latter weeks of Lent and in the Easter season.

Tradition assigns the reading of Isaiah, especially the first part, to Advent. Some texts of this book, however, are read during the Christmas season, to which the First Letter of John is also assigned.

2) The Length of the Texts

75. A *middle way* is followed in regard to the length of texts. A distinction has been made between narratives, which require reading a fairly long passage but which usually hold the attention of the faithful, and texts that should not be lengthy because of the profundity of their doctrine.

In the case of certain rather lengthy texts, longer and shorter versions are provided to suit different situations. The editing of the shorter version has been carried out with great caution.

3) Difficult Texts

76. In readings for Sundays and solemnities, texts that present real difficulties are avoided for pastoral reasons. The difficulties may be objective, in that the texts themselves raise profound literary, critical, or exegetical problems; or the difficulties may lie, at least to a certain extent, in the ability of the faithful to understand the texts. But there could be no justification for concealing from the faithful the spiritual riches of certain texts on the grounds of difficulty if the problem arises from the inadequacy either of the religious education that every Christian should have or of the biblical formation that every pastor of souls should have. Often a difficult reading is clarified by its correlation with another in the same Mass.

4) The Omission of Certain Verses

77. The omission of verses in readings from Scripture has at times been the tradition of many liturgies, including the Roman liturgy. Admittedly such omissions may not be made lightly, for fear of distorting the meaning of the text or the intent and style of Scripture. Yet on pastoral grounds it was decided to continue the traditional practice in the present Order of Readings, but at the same time to ensure that the essential meaning of the text remained intact. One reason for the decision is that otherwise some texts would have been unduly long. It would also have been necessary to omit completely certain readings of high spiritual value for the faithful because those readings include some verse that is pastorally less useful or that involves truly difficult questions.

3. PRINCIPLES TO BE FOLLOWED
IN THE USE OF
THE ORDER OF READINGS

a) The Freedom of Choice Regarding Some Texts

78. The Order of Readings sometimes leaves it to the celebrant to choose between alternative texts or to choose one from the several listed together for the same reading. The option seldom exists on Sundays, solemnities, or feasts, in order not to obscure the character proper to the particular liturgical season or needlessly interrupt the semicontinuous reading of some biblical book. On the other hand, the option is given readily in celebrations of the Saints, in ritual Masses, Masses for various needs and occasions, votive Masses, and Masses for the dead.

These options, together with those indicated in the General Instruction of the Roman Missal and the *Ordo cantus Missae,*[103] have a pastoral purpose. In arranging the liturgy of the word, then, the priest should "consider the general spiritual good of the congregation rather than his personal outlook. He should be mindful that the choice of texts is to be made in harmony with the ministers and others who have a role in the celebration and should listen to the opinions of the faithful in what concerns them more directly."[104]

1) The Two Readings Before the Gospel

79. In Masses to which three readings are assigned, all three are to be used. If, however, for pastoral reasons the Conference of Bishops has given permission for two readings only to be used,[105] the choice between the two first readings is to be made in such a way as to safeguard the Church's intent to instruct the faithful more completely in the mystery of salvation. Thus, unless the contrary is indicated in the text of the Lectionary, the reading to be chosen as the first reading is the one that is more closely in harmony with the Gospel, or, in accord with the intent just mentioned, the one that is more helpful toward a coherent catechesis over an extended period, or that preserves the semicontinuous reading of some biblical book.[106]

2) The Longer and Shorter Forms of Texts

80. A pastoral criterion must also guide the choice between the longer and shorter forms of the same text. The main consideration must be the capacity of the hearers to listen profitably either to the longer or to the shorter reading; or to listen to a more complete text that will be explained through the homily.

3) When Two Texts Are Provided

81. When a choice is allowed between alternative texts, whether they are fixed or optional, the first consideration must be the best interest of those taking part. It may be a matter of using the easier texts or the one more relevant to the assembled congregation or, as pastoral advantage may suggest, of repeating or replacing a text that is assigned as proper to one celebration and optional to another.

The issue may arise when it is feared that some text will create difficulties for a particular congregation or when the same text would have to be repeated within a few days, as on a Sunday and on a day during the week following.

4) The Weekday Readings

82. The arrangement of weekday readings provides texts for every day of the week throughout the year. In most cases, therefore, these readings are to be used on their assigned days, unless a solemnity, a feast, or else a memorial with proper readings occurs.[107]

In using the Order of Readings for weekdays, attention must be paid to whether one reading or another from the same biblical book will have to be omitted because of some celebration occurring during the week. With the arrangement of readings for the entire week in mind, the priest in that case arranges to omit the less significant passages or combines them in the most appropriate manner with other readings, if they contribute to an integral view of a particular theme.

5) The Celebrations of the Saints

83. When they exist, proper readings are given for celebrations of the Saints, that is, biblical passages about the Saint or the mystery that the Mass is celebrating. Even in the case of a memorial these readings must take the place of the weekday readings for the same day. This Order of Readings makes explicit note of every case of proper readings on a memorial.

In some cases there are accommodated readings, those, namely, that bring out some particular aspect of a Saint's spiritual life or work. Use of such readings does not seem binding, except for compelling pastoral reasons. For the most part references are given to readings in the Commons in order to facilitate choice. But these are merely suggestions: in place of an accommodated reading or the particular reading proposed from a Common, any other reading from the Commons referred to may be selected.

The first concern of a priest celebrating with a congregation is the spiritual benefit of the faithful, and he will be careful not to impose his personal preference on them. Above all he will make sure not to omit too often or without sufficient cause the readings assigned for each day in the weekday Lectionary: the Church's desire is that a more lavish table of the word of God be spread before the faithful.[108]

There are also common readings, that is, those placed in the Commons either for some determined class of Saints (martyrs, virgins, pastors) or for the Saints in general. Because in these cases several texts are listed for the same reading, it will be up to the priest to choose the one best suited to those listening.

In all celebrations of Saints, the readings may be taken not only from the Commons to which the references are given in each case, but also from the Common of Men and Women Saints, whenever there is special reason for doing so.

84.   For celebrations of the Saints the following should be observed:

1.   On solemnities and feasts, the readings must be those that are given in the Proper or in the Commons. For solemnities and feasts of the General Roman Calendar proper readings are always assigned.

2.   On solemnities inscribed in particular calendars, three readings are to be assigned, unless the Conference of Bishops has decreed that there are to be only two readings.[109] The first reading is from the Old Testament (but during the Easter season, from the Acts of the Apostles or the Book of Revelation); the second, from an Apostle; the third, from the Gospels.

3.   On feasts and memorials, which have only two readings, the first reading can be chosen from either the Old Testament or from an Apostle; the second is from the Gospels. Following the Church's traditional practice, however, the first reading during the Easter season is to be taken from an Apostle, the second, as far as possible, from the Gospel of John.

6) Other Parts of the Order of Readings

85.   In the Order of Readings for ritual Masses, the references given are to the texts already published for the individual rites. This obviously does not include the texts belonging to celebrations that must not be integrated with Mass.[110]

86.   The Order of Readings for Masses for various needs and occasions, votive Masses, and Masses for the dead provides many texts that can be of assistance in adapting such celebrations to the situation, circumstances, and concerns of the particular groups taking part.[111]

87.   In ritual Masses, Masses for various needs and occasions, votive Masses, and Masses for the dead, since many texts are given for the same reading, the choice of readings follows the criteria already indicated for the choice of readings from the Common of Saints.

88. On a day when some ritual Mass is not permitted and when the norms in the individual rite allow the choice of one reading from those provided for ritual Masses, the general spiritual welfare of the participants must be considered.[112]

b) The Responsorial Psalm and the Acclamation
Before the Gospel Reading

89. Among the chants between the readings, the psalm which follows the first reading is of great importance. As a rule the psalm to be used is the one assigned to the reading. But in the case of readings for the Common of Saints, ritual Masses, Masses for various needs and occasions, votive Masses, and Masses for the dead, the choice is left up to the priest celebrating. He will base his choice on the principle of the pastoral benefit of those present.

But to make it easier for the people to join in the response to the psalm, the Order of Readings lists certain other texts of psalms and responses that have been chosen according to the various seasons or classes of Saints. Whenever the psalm is sung, these texts may replace the text corresponding to the reading.[113]

90. The chant between the second reading and the Gospel is either specified in each Mass and correlated with the Gospel or else it is left as a choice to be made from those in the series given for a liturgical season or one of the Commons.

91. During Lent, one of the acclamations from those given in the Order of Readings may be used, depending on the occasion.[114] This acclamation precedes and follows the verse before the Gospel.

CHAPTER V
DESCRIPTION OF THE
ORDER OF READINGS

92.   It seems useful to provide here a brief description of the Order of Readings, at least for the principal celebrations and the different seasons of the liturgical year. With these in mind, readings were selected on the basis of the rules already stated. This description is meant to assist pastors of souls to understand the structure of the Order of Readings, so that their use of it will become more perceptive and the Order of Readings a source of good for Christ's faithful.

1. ADVENT

a) The Sundays

93.   Each Gospel reading has a distinctive theme: the Lord's coming at the end of time (First Sunday of Advent), John the Baptist (Second and Third Sunday), and the events that prepared immediately for the Lord's birth (Fourth Sunday).

The Old Testament readings are prophecies about the Messiah and the Messianic age, especially from the Book of Isaiah.

The readings from an Apostle contain exhortations and proclamations, in keeping with the different themes of Advent.

b) The Weekdays

94.   There are two series of readings: one to be used from the beginning of Advent until December 16; the other from December 17 to December 24.

In the first part of Advent there are readings from the Book of Isaiah, distributed in accord with the sequence of the book itself and including the more important texts that are also read on the Sundays. For the choice of the weekday Gospel, the first reading has been taken into consideration.

On Thursday of the second week, the readings from the Gospel concerning John the Baptist begin. The first reading is either a continuation of Isaiah or a text chosen in view of the Gospel.

In the last week before Christmas, the events that immediately prepared for the Lord's birth are presented from the Gospels of Matthew (chapter 1) and Luke (chapter 1). The texts in the first reading, chosen in view of the Gospel reading, are from different Old Testament books and include important Messianic prophecies.

2. THE CHRISTMAS SEASON

a) The Solemnities, Feasts, and Sundays

95. For the vigil and the three Masses of Christmas both the prophetic readings and the others have been chosen from the Roman tradition.

The Gospel on the Sunday within the Octave of Christmas, Feast of the Holy Family, is about Jesus' childhood and the other readings are about the virtues of family life.

On the Octave Day of Christmas, Solemnity of the Blessed Virgin Mary, the Mother of God, the readings are about the Virgin Mother of God and the giving of the holy Name of Jesus.

On the Second Sunday after Christmas, the readings are about the mystery of the Incarnation.

On the Epiphany of the Lord, the Old Testament reading and the Gospel continue the Roman tradition; the text for the reading from the Letters of the Apostles is about the calling of the nations to salvation.

On the Feast of the Baptism of the Lord, the texts chosen are about this mystery.

b) The Weekdays

96. From December 29 on, there is a continuous reading of the whole of the First Letter of John, which actually begins earlier, on December 27, the Feast of St. John the Evangelist, and on December 28, the Feast of the Holy Innocents. The Gospels relate manifestations of the Lord: events of Jesus' childhood from the Gospel of Luke (December 29-30); passages from the first chapter of the Gospel of John (December 31-January 5); other manifestations of the Lord from the four Gospels (January 7-12).

3. LENT

a) The Sundays

97. The Gospel readings are arranged as follows:

The first and second Sundays maintain the accounts of the Temptation and Transfiguration of the Lord, with readings, however, from all three Synoptics.

On the next three Sundays, the Gospels about the Samaritan woman, the man born blind, and the raising of Lazarus have been restored in Year

A. Because these Gospels are of major importance in regard to Christian initiation, they may also be read in Year B and Year C, especially in places where there are catechumens.

Other texts, however, are provided for Year B and Year C: for Year B, a text from John about Christ's coming glorification through his Cross and Resurrection and for Year C, a text from Luke about conversion.

On Palm Sunday of the Lord's Passion, the texts for the procession are selections from the Synoptic Gospels concerning the Lord's solemn entry into Jerusalem. For the Mass, the reading is the account of the Lord's Passion.

The Old Testament readings are about the history of salvation, which is one of the themes proper to the catechesis of Lent. The series of texts for each year presents the main elements of salvation history from its beginning until the promise of the New Covenant.

The readings from the Letters of the Apostles have been selected to fit the Gospel and the Old Testament readings and, to the extent possible, to provide a connection between them.

b) The Weekdays

98. The readings from the Gospels and the Old Testament were selected because they are related to each other. They treat various themes of the Lenten catechesis that are suited to the spiritual significance of this season. Beginning with Monday of the Fourth Week of Lent, there is a semicontinuous reading of the Gospel of John, made up of texts that correspond more closely to the themes proper to Lent.

Because the readings about the Samaritan woman, the man born blind, and the raising of Lazarus are now assigned to Sundays, but only for Year A (in Year B and Year C they are optional), provision has been made for their use on weekdays. Thus at the beginning of the Third, Fourth, and Fifth Weeks of Lent optional Masses with these texts for the Gospel have been inserted and may be used in place of the readings of the day on any weekday of the respective week.

In the first days of Holy Week, the readings are about the mystery of Christ's passion. For the Chrism Mass the readings bring out both Christ's Messianic mission and its continuation in the Church by means of the sacraments.

4. THE SACRED TRIDUUM AND THE EASTER SEASON

a) The Sacred Easter Triduum

99. On Holy Thursday at the evening Mass, the remembrance of the meal preceding the Exodus casts its own special light because of Christ's example in washing the feet of his disciples and Paul's account of the institution of the Christian Passover in the Eucharist.

On Good Friday, the liturgical service has as its center John's narrative of the Passion of him who was proclaimed in Isaiah as the Servant of the LORD and who became the one High Priest by offering himself to the Father.

At the Vigil on the holy night of Easter, there are seven Old Testament readings which recall the wonderful works of God in the history of salvation. There are two New Testament readings, the announcement of the Resurrection according to one of the Synoptic Gospels, and a reading from St. Paul on Christian baptism as the sacrament of Christ's Resurrection.

The Gospel reading for the Mass on Easter day is from John on the finding of the empty tomb. There is also, however, the option to use the Gospel texts from the Easter Vigil or, when there is an evening Mass on Easter Sunday, to use the account in Luke of the Lord's appearance to the disciples on the road to Emmaus. The first reading is from the Acts of the Apostles, which throughout the Easter season replaces the Old Testament reading. The reading from the Apostle Paul concerns the living out of the paschal mystery in the Church.

b) The Sundays

100. The Gospel readings for the first three Sundays recount the appearances of the risen Christ. The readings about the Good Shepherd are assigned to the Fourth Sunday. On the Fifth, Sixth, and Seventh Sundays, there are excerpts from the Lord's discourse and prayer at the end of the Last Supper.

The first reading is from the Acts of the Apostles, in a three-year cycle of parallel and progressive selections: material is presented on the life of the early Church, its witness, and its growth.

For the reading from the Apostles, the First Letter of Peter is in Year A, the First Letter of John in Year B, the Book of Revelation in Year C. These are the texts that seem to fit in especially well with the spirit of joyous faith and sure hope proper to this season.

c) The Weekdays

101. As on the Sundays, the first reading is a semicontinuous reading from the Acts of the Apostles. The Gospel readings during the Easter octave are accounts of the Lord's appearances. After that there is a semicontinuous reading of the Gospel of John, but with texts that have a paschal character, in order to complete the reading from John during Lent. This paschal reading is made up in large part of the Lord's discourse and prayer at the end of the Last Supper.

d) The Solemnities of the Ascension and of Pentecost

102. For the first reading the Solemnity of the Ascension retains the account of the Ascension according to the Acts of the Apostles. This text is complemented by the second reading from the Apostle on Christ in exaltation at the right hand of the Father. For the Gospel reading, each of the three years has its own text in accord with the differences in the Synoptic Gospels.

In the evening Mass celebrated on the Vigil of Pentecost, four Old Testament texts are provided; any one of them may be used, in order to bring out the many aspects of Pentecost. The reading from the Apostles shows the actual working of the Holy Spirit in the Church. The Gospel reading recalls the promise of the Spirit made by Christ before his own glorification.

For the Mass on Pentecost day itself, in accord with received usage, the account in the Acts of the Apostles of the great occurrence on Pentecost day is taken as the first reading. The texts from the Apostle Paul bring out the effect of the action of the Spirit in the life of the Church. The Gospel reading is a remembrance of Jesus bestowing his Spirit on the disciples on the evening of Easter day; other optional texts describe the action of the Spirit on the disciples and on the Church.

5. ORDINARY TIME

a) The Arrangement and Choice of Texts

103. Ordinary Time begins on the Monday after the Sunday following January 6; it lasts until the Tuesday before Lent inclusive. It begins again on the Monday after Pentecost Sunday and finishes before evening prayer I of the First Sunday of Advent.

The Order of Readings provides readings for thirty-four Sundays and the weeks following them. In some years, however, there are only thirty-three weeks of Ordinary Time. Further, some Sundays either belong to another season (the Sunday on which the Feast of the Baptism of the Lord falls and Pentecost Sunday) or else are impeded by a solemnity that coincides with Sunday (e.g., The Most Holy Trinity or Christ the King).

104. For the correct arrangement in the use of the readings for Ordinary Time, the following are to be respected.

1. The Sunday on which the Feast of the Baptism of the Lord falls replaces the First Sunday in Ordinary Time. Therefore the readings of the First Week of Ordinary Time begin on the Monday after the Sunday following January 6. When the Feast of the Baptism of the Lord is celebrated on Monday because the Epiphany

has been celebrated on the Sunday, the readings of the First Week begin on Tuesday.

2. The Sunday following the Feast of the Baptism of the Lord is the Second Sunday of Ordinary Time. The remaining Sundays are numbered consecutively up to the Sunday preceding the beginning of Lent. The readings for the week in which Ash Wednesday falls are interrupted after the Tuesday readings.

3. For the resumption of the readings of Ordinary Time after Pentecost Sunday:

—when there are thirty-four Sundays in Ordinary Time, the week to be used is the one that immediately follows the last week used before Lent;[115]

—when there are thirty-three Sundays in Ordinary Time, the first week that would have been used after Pentecost is omitted, in order to reserve for the end of the year the eschatological texts that are assigned to the last two weeks.[116]

b) The Sunday Readings

1) The Gospel Readings

105. On the Second Sunday of Ordinary Time the Gospel continues to center on the manifestation of the Lord, which is celebrated on the Solemnity of the Epiphany, through the traditional passage about the wedding feast at Cana and two other passages from the Gospel of John.

Beginning with the Third Sunday, there is a semicontinuous reading of the Synoptic Gospels. This reading is arranged in such a way that as the Lord's life and preaching unfold the doctrine proper to each of these Gospels is presented.

This distribution also provides a certain coordination between the meaning of each Gospel and the progress of the liturgical year. Thus after Epiphany the readings are on the beginning of the Lord's preaching, and they fit in well with Christ's baptism and the first events in which he manifests himself. The liturgical year leads quite naturally to a conclusion in the eschatological theme proper to the last Sundays, since the chapters of the Synoptics that precede the account of the Passion treat this eschatological theme rather extensively.

After the Sixteenth Sunday in Year B, five readings are incorporated from John chapter 6 (the discourse on the bread of life). This is the natural place for these readings because the multiplication of the loaves from the Gospel of John takes the place of the same account in Mark. In the semicontinuous reading of Luke for Year C, the introduction of this Gospel has been prefixed to the first text (that is, on the Third Sunday). This passage expresses the author's intention very beautifully and there seemed to be no better place for it.

2) The Old Testament Readings

106. These readings have been chosen to correspond to the Gospel passages in order to avoid an excessive diversity between the readings of different Masses and above all to bring out the unity between the Old and the New Testament. The connection between the readings of the same Mass is shown by a precise choice of the readings prefixed to the individual readings.

To the degree possible, the readings were chosen in such a way that they would be short and easy to grasp. But care has been taken to ensure that many Old Testament texts of major significance would be read on Sundays. Such readings are distributed not according to a logical order but on the basis of what the Gospel reading requires. Still, the treasury of the word of God will be opened up in such a way that nearly all the principal pages of the Old Testament will become familiar to those taking part in the Mass on Sundays.

3) The Readings from the Apostles

107. There is a semicontinuous reading of the Letters of Paul and James (the Letters of Peter and John being read during the Easter and Christmas seasons).

Because it is quite long and deals with such diverse issues, the First Letter to the Corinthians has been spread over the three years of the cycle at the beginning of Ordinary Time. It also was thought best to divide the Letter to the Hebrews into two parts; the first part is read in Year B and the second in Year C.

Only readings that are short and readily grasped by the people have been chosen.

Table II at the end of this Introduction[117] indicates the distribution of Letters of the Apostles over the three-year cycle of the Sundays of Ordinary Time.

c) The Readings for Solemnities of the Lord During Ordinary Time

108. On the solemnities of Holy Trinity, Corpus Christi, and the Sacred Heart, the texts chosen correspond to the principal themes of these celebrations.

The readings of the Thirty-Fourth and last Sunday of Ordinary Time celebrate Christ the universal King. He was prefigured by David and proclaimed as king amid the humiliations of his Passion and Cross; he reigns in the Church and will come again at the end of time.

d) The Weekday Readings

109. The *Gospels* are so arranged that Mark is read first (First to Ninth Week), then Matthew (Tenth to Twenty-First Week), then Luke (Twenty-Second to Thirty-Fourth Week). Mark chapters 1-12 are read in their entirety, with the exception only of the two passages of Mark chapter 6 that are read on weekdays in other seasons. From Matthew and Luke the readings comprise all the material not contained in Mark. All the passages that either are distinctively presented in each Gospel or are needed for a proper understanding of its progression are read two or three times. Jesus' eschatological discourse as contained in its entirety in Luke is read at the end of the liturgical year.

110. The *First Reading* is taken in periods of several weeks at a time first from one then from the other Testament; the number of weeks depends on the length of the biblical books read.

Rather large sections are read from the New Testament books in order to give the substance, as it were, of each of the Letters.

From the Old Testament there is room only for select passages that, as far as possible, bring out the character of the individual books. The historical texts have been chosen in such a way as to provide an overall view of the history of salvation before the Incarnation of the Lord. But lengthy narratives could hardly be presented; sometimes verses have been selected that make for a reading of moderate length. In addition, the religious significance of the historical events is sometimes brought out by means of certain texts from the wisdom books that are placed as prologues or conclusions to a series of historical readings.

Nearly all the Old Testament books have found a place in the Order of Readings for weekdays in the Proper of Seasons. The only omissions are the shortest of the prophetic books (Obadiah and Zephaniah) and a poetic book (the Song of Songs). Of those narratives of edification requiring a lengthy reading if they are to be understood, Tobit and Ruth are included, but the others (Esther and Judith) are omitted. Texts from these latter two books are assigned, however, to Sundays and weekdays at other times of the year.

Table III at the end of this Introduction[118] lists the way the books of the Old and the New Testaments are distributed over the weekdays in Ordinary Time in the course of two years.

At the end of the liturgical year the readings are from the books that correspond to the eschatological character of this period, Daniel and the Book of Revelation.

CHAPTER VI
ADAPTATIONS, TRANSLATIONS, AND FORMAT
OF THE ORDER OF READINGS

1. ADAPTATIONS AND TRANSLATIONS

111. In the liturgical assembly, the word of God must always be read either from the Latin texts prepared by the Holy See or from vernacular translations approved for liturgical use by the Conferences of Bishops, according to existing norms.[119]

112. The Lectionary for Mass must be translated integrally in all its parts, including the Introduction. If the Conference of Bishops has judged it necessary and useful to add certain adaptations, these are to be incorporated after their confirmation by the Holy See.[120]

113. The size of the Lectionary will necessitate editions in more than one volume; no particular division of the volumes is prescribed. But each volume is to contain the explanatory texts on the structure and purpose of the section it contains.

The ancient custom is recommended of having separate books, one for the Gospels and the other for the other readings for the Old and New Testaments.

It may also be useful to publish separately a Sunday lectionary (which could also contain selected excerpts from the sanctoral cycle), and a weekday lectionary. A practical basis for dividing the Sunday lectionary is the three-year cycle, so that all the readings for each year are presented in sequence.

But there is freedom to adopt other arrangements that may be devised and seem to have pastoral advantages.

114. The texts for the chants are always to be adjoined to the readings, but separate books containing the chants alone are permitted. It is recommended that the texts be printed with divisions into stanzas.

115. Whenever a text consists of different parts, the typography must make this structure of the text clear. It is likewise recommended that even non-poetic texts be printed with division into sense lines to assist the proclamation of the readings.

116. Where there are longer and shorter forms of a text, they are to be printed separately, so that each can be read with ease. But if such a separation does not seem feasible, a way is to be found to ensure that each text can be proclaimed without mistakes.

117. In vernacular editions, the texts are not to be printed without headings prefixed. If it seems advisable, an introductory note on the general meaning of the passage may be added to the heading. This note is to carry some distinctive symbol or is to be set in different type to show clearly that it is an optional text.[121]

118. It would be useful for every volume to have an index of the passages of the Bible, modeled on the biblical index of the present volume.[122] This will provide ready access to texts of the lectionaries for Mass that may be needed or helpful for specific occasions.

2. THE FORMAT OF INDIVIDUAL READINGS

For each reading the present volume carries the textual reference, the headings, and the *incipit*.

a) The Biblical References

119. The text reference (that is, to chapter and verses) is always given according to the Neo-Vulgate edition for the psalms.[123] But a second reference according to the original text (Hebrew, Aramaic, or Greek) has been added wherever there is a discrepancy. Depending on the decrees of the competent Authorities for the individual languages, vernacular versions may retain the enumeration corresponding to the version of the Bible approved for liturgical use by the same Authorities. Exact references to chapter and verses, however, must always appear and may be given in the text or in the margin.

120. These references provide liturgical books with the basis of the "announcement" of the text that must be read in the celebration, but which is not printed in this volume. This "announcement" of the text will observe the following norms, but they may be altered by decree of the competent authorities on the basis of what is customary and useful for different places and languages.

121. The formula to be used is always: "A *reading* from the Book of . . . ," "A *reading* from the Letter of . . . ," or "A *reading* from the holy Gospel according to . . . ," and not: "The *beginning* of . . . ," (unless this seems advisable in particular instances), nor: "The *continuation* of. . . ."

122. The traditionally accepted titles for books are to be retained with the following exceptions.

1. Where there are two books with the same name, the title is to be: The first Book, The second Book (for example, of Kings, of Maccabees) or The first Letter, The second Letter.

2. The title more common in current usage is to be accepted for the following books:
   — I and II Samuel instead of I and II Kings;
   — I and II Kings instead of III and IV Kings;
   — I and II Chronicles instead of I and II Paralipomenon;
   — The Books of Ezra and Nehemiah instead of I and II Ezra.

3. The distinguishing titles for the wisdom books are: The Book of Job, the Book of Proverbs, the Book of Ecclesiastes, the Song of Songs, the Book of Wisdom, and the Book of Sirach.

4. For all the books that are included among the prophets in the Neo-Vulgate, the formula is to be: "A reading from the Book of the prophet Isaiah, or of the prophet Jeremiah, or of the prophet Baruch" and: "A reading from the Book of the prophet Ezekiel, of the prophet Daniel, of the prophet Hosea, of the prophet Malachi," even in the case of books not regarded by some as being in actual fact prophetic.

5. The title is to be Book of Lamentations and Letter to the Hebrews, with no mention of Jeremiah or Paul.

b) The Heading

123. There is a *heading* prefixed to each text, chosen carefully (usually from the words of the text itself) in order to point out the main theme of the reading and, when necessary, to make the connection between the readings of the same Mass clear.

c) The "Incipit"

124. In this Order of Readings the first element of the *incipit* is the customary introductory phrase: "At that time," "In those days," "Brothers and Sisters," "Beloved," "Dearly Beloved," "Dearest Brothers and Sisters," or "Thus says the Lord," "Thus says the Lord God." These words are not given when the text itself provides sufficient indication of the time or the persons involved or where such phrases would not fit in with the very nature of the text. For the individual languages, such phrases may be changed or omitted by decree of the competent Authorities.

After the first words of the *incipit,* the Order of Readings gives the proper beginning of the reading, with some words deleted or supplied for intelligibility, inasmuch as the text is separated from its context. When the text for a reading is made up of non-consecutive verses and this has required changes in wording, these are appropriately indicated.

d) The Final Acclamation

125. In order to facilitate the congregation's acclamation, the words for the reader *The word of the Lord*, or similar words suited to local custom, are to be printed at the end of the reading for use by the reader.

NOTES

1. Cf. especially Second Vatican Council, *Constitution on the Sacred Liturgy (Sacrosanctum Concilium)*, nos. 7, 24, 33, 35, 48, 51, 52, 56; *Dogmatic Constitution on Divine Revelation (Dei Verbum)*, nos. 1, 21, 25, 26; *Decree on the Missionary Activity of the Church (Ad gentes)*, no. 6; *Decree on the Ministry and Life of Priests (Presbyterorum Ordinis)*, no. 18.

2. Among the spoken or written statements of the Supreme Pontiffs, see especially: Paul VI, Motu Proprio, *Ministeria quaedam*, August 15, 1972, no. V: *Acta Apostolicae Sedis [AAS]* 64 (1972): 532; Apostolic Exhortation, *Marialis cultus*, February 2, 1974, no. 12: *AAS* 66 (1974): 125-126; Apostolic Exhortation, *Evangelii nuntiandi*, December 8, 1975, no. 28: *AAS* 68 (1976): 24-25, no. 43: ibid., pp. 33-34, no. 47: ibid., pp. 36-37; John Paul II, Apostolic Constitution, *Scripturarum thesaurus*, April 25, 1979 in *Nova Vulgata Bibliorum Sacrorum editione*, Typis Polyglottis Vaticanis 1979, pp. V-VIII; Apostolic Exhortation, *Catechesi tradendae*, October 16, 1979, nos. 23, 27, 48: *AAS* 71 (1979): 1296-1297, 1298-1299, 1316; Letter, *Dominicae cenae*, February 24, 1980, no. 10: *AAS* 72 (1980): 134-137.

3. Cf. Sacred Congregation of Rites, Instruction, *Eucharisticum mysterium*, May 25, 1967, no. 10: *AAS* 59 (1967): 547-548; Sacred Congregation for Divine Worship, Instruction, *Liturgicae instaurationes*, September 5, 1970, no. 2: *AAS* 62 (1970): 695-696; Sacred Congregation for the Clergy, *Directorum catechesticum generale*, April 11, 1971: *AAS* 64 (1972): 106-107; no. 25: ibid., p. 114; Sacred Congregation for Divine Worship, *Institutio Generalis Missalis Romani*, nos. 9, 11, 24, 33, 60, 62, 316, 320; Sacred Congregation for Catholic Education, Instruction on liturgical formation in seminaries, *In ecclesiasticam futurorum sacerdotum*, June 3, 1979, nos. 11, 52; ibid., Appendix, no. 15; Sacred Congregation for the Sacraments and Divine Worship, Instruction, *Inaestimabile donum*, April 3, 1980, nos. 1, 2, 3: *AAS* 72 (1980): 333-334.

4. Cf. Missale Romanum ex Decreto Sacrosancti Oecumenici Concilii Vaticani II instauratum auctoritate Pauli VI promulgatum, *Ordo lectionum missae* (Typis Polyglottis Vaticanis, 1969) pp. IX-XII (Praenotanda); Decree of promulgation: *AAS* 61 (1969): 548-549.

5. Cf. Second Vatican Council, *Constitution on the Sacred Liturgy (Sacrosanctum Concilium)*, nos. 35, 56; Paul VI, Apostolic Exhortation, *Evangelii nuntiandi*, December 8, 1975, nos. 28, 47: *AAS* 68 (1976): 24-25, 36-37; Letter, *Dominicae cenae*, February 24, 1980, nos. 10, 11, 12: *AAS* 72 (1980): 134-146.

6. For example, the terms "word of God," "Sacred Scripture," "Old" and "New Testament," "Reading (readings) of the word of God," "Reading (readings) from Sacred Scripture," "Celebration (celebrations) of the word of God," etc.

7. Thus one and the same text may be read or used for various reasons on various occasions and celebrations of the Church's liturgical year. This is to be recalled in the homily, in pastoral exegesis, and in catechesis. The indexes of this volume will show, for example, that Romans chapter 6 or Romans chapter 8 is used

in various seasons of the liturgical year and in various celebrations of the sacraments and sacramentals.

8. Cf. Lk 4:6-21; 24:25-35, 44-49.

9. Thus, for example, in the celebration of Mass, there is proclamation, reading, etc. (cf. *Institutio Generalis Missalis Romani*, nos. 21, 23, 95, 131, 146, 234, 235). There are also other celebrations of the word of God in the *Pontificale Romanum*, the *Rituale Romanum*, and the *Liturgia Horarum*, as restored by decree of Second Vatican Council.

10. Cf. Second Vatican Council, *Constitution on the Sacred Liturgy (Sacrosanctum Concilium)*, nos. 7, 33; Mk 16:19-20; Mt 28:20; St. Augustine, *Sermo* 85, 1: "The Gospel is the mouth of Christ. He is seated in heaven yet does not cease to speak on earth" *PL* 38, 520; cf. also *In Io. Ev. tract.* XXX, 1: *PL* 35, 1632; *CCL* 36, 289; *Pontificale Romano-Germanicum*: "The Gospel is read, in which Christ speaks by his own mouth to the people. . . . The Gospel resounds in the church as though Christ himself were speaking to the people" (see C. Vogel and R. Elze, eds., *Le Pontifical romano-germanique du dixième siècle. Le Texte I*, Ciottà del Vaticano, 1963, XCIV, 18, p. 334); or "At the approach of Christ, that is the Gospel, we put aside our staffs, because we have no need of human assistance" (ibid., XCIV, 23, p. 335).

11. Cf. Second Vatican Council, *Constitution on the Sacred Liturgy (Sacrosanctum Concilium)*, no. 7.

12. Cf. Heb 4:12.

13. Cf. St. Augustine, *Quaestionum in Heptateuchum liber* 2, 73: *PL* 34, 623; *CCL* 33, 106; Second Vatican Council, *Dogmatic Constitution on Divine Revelation (Dei Verbum)*, no. 16.

14. Cf. St. Jerome: "If, as St. Paul says (1 Cor 1:24), Christ is the power of God and the wisdom of God, anyone who is ignorant of the Scriptures, is ignorant of the power of God and his wisdom. For ignorance of the Scriptures is ignorance of Christ" (*Commentarii in Isaiam prophetam, Prologus: PL* 24, 17A; *CCL* 73, 1); Second Vatican Council, *Dogmatic Constitution on Divine Revelation (Dei Verbum)*, no. 25.

15. Cf. 2 Cor 1:20-22.

16. Cf. Second Vatican Council, *Constitution on the Sacred Liturgy (Sacrosanctum Concilium)*, no. 10.

17. Cf. 2 Thes 3:1.

18. Cf. *Collectae, Pro Sancta Ecclesia*, in *Missale Romanum ex Decreto Sacrosancti Oecumenici Concilii Vaticani II instauratum auctoritate Pauli VI promulgatum* (Typis Polyglottis Vaticanis, 1975) pp. 786, 787, 790: St. Cyprian, *De oratione dominica* 23: *PL* 4, 553; *CSEL* 3/2, 285; *CCL* 3A, 105; St. Augustine, *Sermo* 71, 20, 33: *PL* 38, 463f.

19. Cf. *Collecta, Dominica XXI "per annum,"* in *Missale Romanum*, p. 360.

20. Cf. Second Vatican Council, *Dogmatic Constitution on Divine Revelation (Dei Verbum)*, no. 8.

21. Cf. Jn 14:15-17, 25-26; 16:15.

22. Second Vatican Council, *Decree on the Ministry and Life of Priests (Presbyterorum Ordinis)*, no. 4.

23. Cf. Second Vatican Council, *Constitution on the Sacred Liturgy (Sacrosanctum Concilium)*, no. 51; *Decree on the Ministry and Life of Priests (Presbyterorum Ordinis)*, no. 18; also *Dogmatic Constitution on Divine Revelation (Dei Verbum)*, no. 21; *Decree on the Missionary Activity of the Church (Ad gentes)*, no. 6. Cf. *Institutio Generalis Missalis Romani*, no. 8.

24. Second Vatican Council, *Constitution on the Sacred Liturgy* (*Sacrosanctum Concilium*), no. 56.

25. *Institutio Generalis Missalis Romani*, no. 33.

26. Cf. Sacred Congregation for Divine Worship, Instruction, *Liturgicae instaurationes*, September 5, 1970, no. 2: *AAS* 62 (1970): 695-696; John Paul II, Letter, *Dominicae cenae*, February 24, 1980, no. 10: *AAS* 72 (1980): 134-137; Sacred Congregation for the Sacraments and Divine Worship, Instruction, *Inaestimabile donum*, April 3, 1980, no. 1: *AAS* 72 (1980): 333.

27. Second Vatican Council, *Constitution on the Sacred Liturgy* (*Sacrosanctum Concilium*), no. 33.

28. Cf. below, no. 111 of this Introduction.

29. Cf. *Missale Romanum ex Decreto Sacrosancti Oecumenici Concilii Vaticani II instauratum auctoritate Pauli VI promulgatum, Ordo cantus Missae*, editio typica 1972, *Praenotanda*, nos. 4, 6, 10.

30. Cf. *Institutio Generalis Missalis Romani*, no. 11.

31. Cf. ibid., no. 272; and nos. 32-34 of this Introduction.

32. Cf. ibid., nos. 35, 95.

33. Cf. ibid., nos. 82-84.

34. Cf. ibid., nos. 94, 131.

35. Cf. *Ordo Missae cum populo*, 11, in: *Missale Romanum ex Decreto Sacrosancti Oecumenici Concilii Vaticani II instauratum auctoritate Pauli VI promulgatum* (Typis Polyglottis Vaticanis, 1975) p. 388.

36. *Institutio Generalis Missalis Romani*, no. 36.

37. Paul VI, Apostolic Constitution, *Laudis canticum* in *Liturgia Horarum ex Decreto Sacrosancti Oecumenici Concilii Vaticani II instaurata auctoritate Pauli VI promulgata* (Typis Polyglottis Vaticanis, 1971); cf. also Second Vatican Council, *Constitution on the Sacred Liturgy* (*Sacrosanctum Concilium*), nos. 24, 90; Sacred Congregation of Rites, Instruction, *Musicam sacram*, March 5, 1967, no. 39: *AAS* 59 (1967): 311; *Liturgia horarum, Instituto Generalis*, nos. 23, 109; Sacred Congregation for Catholic Education, *Ratio fundamentalis*, no. 53.

38. Cf. below, nos. 89-90 of this Introduction.

39. Cf. *Institutio Generalis Missalis Romani*, nos. 18, 38.

40. Cf. ibid., no. 272; and below, no. 32ff. of this Introduction.

41. Cf. ibid., no. 39.

42. Cf. ibid., nos. 37-39; *Missale Romanum ex Decreto Sacrosancti Oecumenici Concilii Vaticani II instauratum auctoritate Pauli VI promulgatum, Ordo cantus Missae, Praenotanda*, nos. 7-9; *Graduale Romanum*, 1974, *Praenotanda*, no. 7; *Graduale simplex*, editio typica altera 1975, *Praenotanda*, no. 16.

43. Second Vatican Council, *Constitution on the Sacred Liturgy* (*Sacrosanctum Concilium*), no. 52; Sacred Congregation of Rites, Instruction, *Inter oecumenici*, September 26, 1964, no. 54: *AAS* 56 (1964): 890.

44. Cf. *Institutio Generalis Missalis Romani*, no. 42.

45. Second Vatican Council, *Constitution on the Sacred Liturgy* (*Sacrosanctum Concilium*), nos. 35, 2.

46. Cf. Second Vatican Council, *Constitution on the Sacred Liturgy* (*Sacrosanctum Concilium*), nos. 6 and 47.

47. Cf. Paul VI, Encyclical, *Mysterium Fidei*, September 3, 1965, no. 36: *AAS* 57 (1965): 753; Second Vatican Council, *Decree on the Missionary Activity of*

the Church (Ad gentes), no. 9; Paul VI, Apostolic Exhortation, *Evangelii nuntiandi*, no. 43: *AAS* 69 (1976): 33-34.

48. Cf. Second Vatican Council, *Constitution on the Sacred Liturgy (Sacrosanctum Concilium)*, nos. 35, 2; *Institutio Generalis Missalis Romani*, no. 41.

49. Second Vatican Council, *Constitution on the Sacred Liturgy (Sacrosanctum Concilium)*, no. 10.

50. Cf. John Paul II, Apostolic Exhortation, *Catechesi tradendae*, October 16, 1979, no. 48: *AAS* 71 (1979): 1316.

51. Cf. *Institutio Generalis Missalis Romani*, no. 165.

52. Cf. ibid., no. 42; and also Sacred Congregation of Rites, Instruction, *Eucharisticum mysterium*, May 25, 1967, no. 28: *AAS* 59 (1967): 556-557.

53. Cf. Sacred Congregation for Divine Worship, Instruction, *Actio pastoralis*, May 15, 1969, no. 6g: *AAS* 61 (1969): 809; *Directorium de Missis cum pueris*, November 1, 1973, no. 48: *AAS* 66 (1974): 44.

54. Cf. *Institutio Generalis Missalis Romani*, nos. 42, 338; *Rituale Romanum ex Decreto Sacrosancti Oecumenici Concilii Vaticani II instauratum, auctoritate Pauli VI promulgatum, Ordo celebrandi Matrimonium* (Typis Polyglottis Vaticanis, 1969), nos. 22, 42, 57; *Ordo Exsequiarum* (Typis Polyglottis Vaticanis, 1969), nos. 41-64.

55. Cf. *Institutio Generalis Missalis Romani*, no. 97.

56. Cf. ibid., no. 139.

57. Cf. ibid., no. 23.

58. Cf. ibid., no. 43.

59. Cf. ibid., no. 45.

60. Cf. ibid., no. 99.

61. Cf. ibid., no. 47.

62. Cf. above, no. 23 of this Introduction.

63. Cf. *Institutio Generalis Missalis Romani*, no. 272.

64. Cf. Second Vatican Council, *Constitution on the Sacred Liturgy (Sacrosanctum Concilium)*, no. 122.

65. Cf. *Pontificale Romanum ex Decreto Sacrosancti Oecumenici Concilii Vaticani II instauratum auctoritate Pauli VI promulgatum, De Ordinatione Diaconi, Presbyteri et Episcopi* (Typis Polyglottis Vaticanis, 1968) p. 28, no. 24; p. 68, no. 21; p. 85, no. 24; p. 70, no. 25; p. 100, no. 25.

66. Cf. below, nos. 78-91 of this Introduction.

67. Cf. *Institutio Generalis Missalis Romani*, nos. 318-320, 324-325.

68. Cf. ibid., no. 313.

69. Cf. ibid., no. 42; Sacred Congregation for the Sacraments and Divine Worship, Instruction, *Inaestimabile donum*, no. 3: *AAS* 72 (1980): 334.

70. Cf. *Institutio Generalis Missalis Romani*, no. 11.

71. Cf. ibid., no. 68.

72. Cf. ibid., nos. 33, 47.

73. Second Vatican Council, *Decree on the Ministry and Life of Priests (Presbyterorum Ordinis)*, no. 4.

74. Second Vatican Council, *Constitution on the Sacred Liturgy (Sacrosanctum Concilium)*, no. 33.

75. Cf. *Institutio Generalis Missalis Romani*, no. 9.

76. Second Vatican Council, *Constitution on the Sacred Liturgy (Sacrosanctum Concilium)*, no. 7.

77. Cf. ibid., no. 9.

78. Cf. Rom 1:16.

79. Cf. Second Vatican Council, *Dogmatic Constitution on Divine Revelation (Dei Verbum)*, no. 21.

80. Quoted ibid.

81. Cf. Jn 14:15-26; 15:26–16:4, 5-15.

82. Cf. Second Vatican Council, *Decree on the Missionary Activity of the Church (Ad gentes)*, nos. 6 and 15; and also *Dogmatic Constitution on Divine Revelation (Dei Verbum)*, no. 26.

83. Cf. Second Vatican Council, *Constitution on the Sacred Liturgy (Sacrosanctum Concilium)*, no. 24; and also Sacred Congregation for the Clergy, *Directorium catecheticum generale*, April 11, 1971, no. 25: *AAS* 64 (1972): 114.

84. Cf. Second Vatican Council, *Constitution on the Sacred Liturgy (Sacrosanctum Concilium)*, no. 56; see also Sacred Congregation for the Sacraments and Divine Worship, Instruction, *Inaestimabile donum*, April 3, 1980, no. 1: *AAS* 72 (1980): 333-334.

85. Cf. Second Vatican Council, *Constitution on the Sacred Liturgy (Sacrosanctum Concilium)*, nos. 24 and 35.

86. Cf. *Institutio Generalis Missalis Romani*, no. 34.

87. Cf. ibid., no. 96.

88. Cf. ibid., nos. 47, 61, 132; Sacred Congregation for the Sacraments and Divine Worship, Instruction, *Inaestimabile donum*, April 3, 1980, no. 3: *AAS* 72 (1980): 334.

89. Cf. *Institutio Generalis Missalis Romani*, no. 66.

90. Cf. Paul VI, Motu Proprio, *Ministeria quaedam*, August 15, 1972, no. V: *AAS* 64 (1972): 532.

91. Cf. Sacred Congregation for the Sacraments and Divine Worship, Instruction, *Inaestimabile donum*, nos. 2 and 18: *AAS* 72 (1980): 334; cf. also Sacred Congregation for Divine Worship, *Directorium de Missis cum pueris*, November 1, 1973, nos. 22, 24, 27: *AAS* 66 (1974): 43.

92. Cf. *Institutio Generalis Missalis Romani*, nos. 47, 66, 151; cf. also Consilium ad exsequendam Constitutionem de sacra Liturgia, *De oratione communi fidelium* (Città del Vaticano, 1966), no. 8.

93. Cf. *Institutio Generalis Missalis Romani*, no. 66.

94. Cf. ibid., nos. 37a and 67.

95. Cf. ibid., no. 68.

96. Cf, for example, Pope Paul VI, Apostolic Constitution, *Missale Romanum*, April 3, 1969, in *Missale Romanum ex Decreto Sacrosancti Oecumenici Concilii Vaticani II instauratum auctoritate Pauli VI promulgatum* (Typis Polyglottis Vaticanis, 1975), p. 15, quoted in *Missale Romanum ex Decreto Sacrosancti Oecumenici Concilii Vaticani II instauratum auctoritate Pauli VI promulgatum, Ordo lectionum Missae*, editio typica altera (Typis Polyglottis Vaticanis, 1981), p. XXX.

97. Cf. Second Vatican Council, *Constitution on the Sacred Liturgy (Sacrosanctum Concilium)*, nos. 35 and 51.

98. Cf. Pope Paul VI, Apostolic Constitution, *Missale Romanum*: in *Missale Romanum ex Decreto Sacrosancti Oecumenici Concilii Vaticani II instauratum auctoritate Pauli VI promulgatum* (Typis Polyglottis Vaticanis, 1975), p. 15, quoted

in *Missale Romanum ex Decreto Sacrosancti Oecumenici Concilii Vaticani II instauratum auctoritate Pauli VI promulgatum, Ordo lectionum Missae*, editio typica altera (Typis Polyglottis Vaticanis, 1981), p. XXXI.

99. Cf. Second Vatican Council, *Constitution on the Sacred Liturgy (Sacrosanctum Concilium)*, nos. 9 and 33; Sacred Congregation of Rites, Instruction, *Inter oecumenici*, September 26, 1964, no. 7: *AAS* 56 (1964): 878; John Paul II, Apostolic Exhortation, *Catechesi tradendae*, October 16, 1979, no. 23: *AAS* 71 (1979): 1296-1297.

100. Cf. Second Vatican Council, *Constitution on the Sacred Liturgy (Sacrosanctum Concilium)*, nos. 35, 4; Sacred Congregation of Rites, Instruction, *Inter oecumenici*, September 26, 1964, nos. 37-38: *AAS* 56 (1964): 884.

101. Cf. Sacred Congregation for Divine Worship, Instruction, *Actio pastoralis*, May 15, 1969, no. 6: *AAS* 61 (1969): 809; Sacred Congregation for Divine Worship, *Directorium de Missis cum pueris*, November 1, 1973, nos. 41-47: *AAS* 66 (1974): 43; Paul VI, Apostolic Exhortation *Marialis cultus*, February 2, 1974, no. 12: *AAS* 66 (1974): 125-126.

102. Each of the years is designated by the letter A, B, or C. The following is the procedure to determine which year is A, B, or C. The letter C designates a year whose number is divisible into three equal parts, as though the cycle had taken its beginning from the first year of the Christian era. Thus the year 1 would have been Year A; year 2, Year B; year 3, Year C (as would years 6, 9, and 12). Thus, for example, year 1980 is Year C; 1981, Year A; 1982, Year B; and 1983, Year C again. And so forth. Obviously each cycle runs in accord with the plan of the liturgical year, that is, it begins with the First Week of Advent, which falls in the preceding year of the civil calendar.

The years in each cycle are marked in a sense by the principal characteristic of the Synoptic Gospel used for the semicontinuous reading of Ordinary Time. Thus the first year of the cycle is the year for the reading of the Gospel of Matthew and is so named; the second and third years are the year of Mark and the year of Luke.

103. Cf. *Institutio Generalis Missalis Romani*, nos. 36-40; *Missale Romanum ex Decreto Sacrosancti Oecumenici Concilii Vaticani II instauratum auctoritate Pauli VI promulgatum, Ordo cantus Missae* (Typis Polyglottis Vaticanis), nos. 5-9.

104. Cf. *Institutio Generalis Missalis Romani*, no. 313.

105. Cf. ibid., no. 318; Sacred Congregation for the Sacraments and Divine Worship, Instruction, *Inaestimabile donum*, no. 1: *AAS* 72 (1980): 333-334.

106. For example: In Lent the continuity of the Old Testament readings corresponds to the unfolding of the history of salvation; the Sundays in Ordinary Time provide the semicontinuous reading of one of the Letters of the Apostles. In these cases it is right that the pastor of souls choose one or other of the readings in a systematic way over a series of Sundays, so that he may establish a coherent plan for catechesis. It is not right to read indiscriminately on one day from the Old Testament, on another from the Letter of an Apostle, without any orderly plan for the texts that follow.

107. Cf. *Institutio Generalis Missalis Romani*, no. 319.

108. Cf. ibid., no. 316c; see Second Vatican Council, *Constitution on the Sacred Liturgy (Sacrosanctum Concilium)*, no. 51.

109. Cf. *Institutio Generalis Missalis Romani*, no. 318.

110. Cf. *Rituale Romanum ex Decreto Sacrosancti Oecumenici Concilii Vaticani II instauratum, auctoritate Pauli VI promulgatum, Ordo Paenitentiae* (Typis Polyglottis Vaticanis, 1974) *Praenotanda*, no. 13.

111. Cf. *Institutio Generalis Missalis Romani*, no. 320.

112. Cf. ibid., no. 313.

113. Cf. nos. 173-174 of this Order of Readings.

114. Cf. no. 233 of this Order of Readings.

115. So, for example, when there are six weeks before Lent, the seventh week begins on the Monday after Pentecost. The Solemnity of the Most Holy Trinity replaces the Sunday of Ordinary Time.

116. When there are, for example, five weeks before Lent, the Monday after Pentecost begins with the Seventh Week of Ordinary Time and the Sixth Week is omitted.

117. Cf. Table II at the end of this Introduction.

118. Cf. Table III at the end of this Introduction.

119. Cf. *Missale Romanum ex Decreto Sacrosancti Oecumenici Concilii Vaticani II instauratum auctoritate Pauli VI promulgatum, Ordo lectionum Missae*, editio typica altera (Typis Polyglottis Vaticanis, 1981), p. XLVII, no. 119.

120. Cf. Sacred Congregation for Divine Worship, Instruction, *Liturgicae instaurationes*, September 5, 1970, no. 11: *AAS* 62 (1970): 702-703; *Institutio Generalis Missalis Romani*, no. 325.

121. Cf. ibid., *IGRM*, nos. 11, 29, 68a, 139.

122. Cf. Index of Readings of this Order of Readings.

123. The references for the psalms follow the order of the *Liber Psalmorum*, published by the Pontifical Commission for the Neo-Vulgate (Typis Polyglottis Vaticanis, 1969).

TABLE I
PRINCIPAL CELEBRATIONS
OF THE LITURGICAL YEAR

Year	Lectionary Cycle Sunday/Weekday	Ash Wednesday	Easter	Ascension Thursday	Pentecost
1998	C/II	Feb 25	Apr 12	May 21	May 31
1999	A/I	Feb 17	Apr 4	May 13	May 23
2000	B/II	Mar 8	Apr 23	June 1	June 11
2001	C/I	Feb 28	Apr 15	May 24	June 3
2002	A/II	Feb 13	Mar 31	May 9	May 19
2003	B/I	Mar 5	Apr 20	May 29	June 8
2004	C/II	Feb 25	Apr 11	May 20	May 30
2005	A/I	Feb 9	Mar 27	May 5	May 15
2006	B/II	Mar 1	Apr 16	May 25	June 4
2007	C/I	Feb 21	Apr 8	May 17	May 27
2008	A/II	Feb 6	Mar 23	May 1	May 11
2009	B/I	Feb 25	Apr 12	May 21	May 31
2010	C/II	Feb 17	Apr 4	May 13	May 23
2011	A/I	Mar 9	Apr 24	June 2	June 12
2012	B/II	Feb 22	Apr 8	May 17	May 27
2013	C/I	Feb 13	Mar 31	May 9	May 19
2014	A/II	Mar 5	Apr 20	May 29	June 8
2015	B/I	Feb 18	Apr 5	May 14	May 24
2016	C/II	Feb 10	Mar 27	May 5	May 15
2017	A/I	Mar 1	Apr 16	May 25	June 4
2018	B/II	Feb 14	Apr 1	May 10	May 20
2019	C/I	Mar 6	Apr 21	May 30	June 9
2020	A/II	Feb 26	Apr 12	May 21	May 31
2021	B/I	Feb 17	Apr 4	May 13	May 23
2022	C/II	Mar 2	Apr 17	May 26	Jun 5
2023	A/I	Feb 22	Apr 9	May 18	May 28
2024	B/II	Feb 14	Mar 31	May 9	May 19
2025	C/I	Mar 5	Apr 20	May 29	June 8

TABLE I (continued)

| | | Weeks in Ordinary Time | | | | |
| | | before Lent | | after Easter Season | | |
Year	Lectionary Cycle Sunday/Weekday	Number of Weeks	Ending	Beginning	Week Number	First Sunday of Advent
1998	C/II	7	Feb 24	June 1	9	Nov 29
1999	A/I	6	Feb 16	May 24	8	Nov 28
2000	B/II	9	Mar 7	June 12	10	Dec 3
2001	C/I	7	Feb 27	June 1	9	Dec 2
2002	A/II	5	Feb 12	May 20	7	Dec 1
2003	B/I	8	Mar 4	June 9	10	Nov 30
2004	C/II	7	Feb 24	May 31	9	Nov 28
2005	A/I	5	Feb 8	May 16	7	Nov 27
2006	B/II	8	Feb 28	June 5	9	Dec 3
2007	C/I	7	Feb 20	May 28	8	Dec 2
2008	A/II	4	Feb 5	May 12	6	Nov 30
2009	B/I	7	Feb 24	June 1	9	Nov 29
2010	C/II	6	Feb 16	May 24	8	Nov 28
2011	A/I	9	Mar 8	June 13	11	Nov 27
2012	B/II	7	Feb 21	May 28	8	Dec 2
2013	C/I	5	Feb 12	May 20	7	Dec 1
2014	A/II	8	Mar 4	June 9	10	Nov 30
2015	B/I	6	Feb 17	May 25	8	Nov 29
2016	C/II	5	Feb 9	May 16	7	Nov 27
2017	A/I	8	Feb 28	June 5	9	Dec 3
2018	B/II	6	Feb 13	May 21	7	Dec 2
2019	C/I	8	Mar 5	June 10	10	Dec 1
2020	A/II	7	Feb 25	June 1	9	Nov 29
2021	B/I	6	Feb 16	May 24	8	Nov 28
2022	C/II	8	Mar 1	June 6	10	Nov 27
2023	A/I	7	Feb 21	May 29	8	Dec 3
2024	B/II	6	Feb 13	May 20	7	Dec 1
2025	C/I	8	Mar 4	June 9	10	Nov 30

TABLE II
ORDER OF THE SECOND READING
FOR SUNDAYS IN ORDINARY TIME

Sunday	Year A	Year B	Year C
2	1 Cor 1–4	1 Cor 6–11	1 Cor 12–15
3	"	"	"
4	"	"	"
5	"	"	"
6	"	"	"
7	"	2 Cor	"
8	"	"	"
9	Rom	"	Gal
10	"	"	"
11	"	"	"
12	"	"	"
13	"	"	"
14	"	"	"
15	"	Eph	Col
16	"	"	"
17	"	"	"
18	"	"	"
19	"	"	Heb 11–12
20	"	"	"
21	"	"	"
22	"	Jas	"
23	"	"	Phlm
24	"	"	1 Tm
25	Phil	"	"
26	"	"	"
27	"	Heb 1–10	2 Tm
28	"	"	"
29	1 Thes	"	"
30	"	"	"
31	"	"	2 Thes
32	"	"	"
33	"	"	"

TABLE III
ORDER OF THE FIRST READING
FOR WEEKDAYS IN ORDINARY TIME

Week	Year I	Year II
1	Heb	1 Sm
2	"	"
3	"	2 Sm
4	"	2 Sm; 1 Kgs, 1–16
5	Gn, 1–11	1 Kgs, 1–16
6	"	Jas
7	Sir	"
8	"	1 Pt; Jude
9	Tb	2 Pt; 2 Tm
10	2 Cor	1 Kgs, 17–22
11	"	1 Kgs, 17–22; 2 Kgs
12	Gn, 12–50	2 Kgs; Lam
13	"	Am
14	"	Hos; Is
15	Ex	Is; Mi
16	"	Mi; Jer
17	Ex; Lv	Jer
18	Nm; Dt	Jer; Na; Hb
19	Dt; Jos	Ez
20	Jgs; Ru	"
21	1 Thes	2 Thes; 1 Cor
22	1 Thes; Col	1 Cor
23	Col; 1 Tm	"
24	1 Tm	"
25	Ezr; Hg; Zec	Prv; Sir
26	Zec; Neh; Bar	Jb
27	Jon; Mal; Jl	Gal
28	Rom	Gal; Eph
29	"	Eph
30	"	"
31	"	Eph; Phil
32	Wis	Ti; Phlm; 2 and 3 Jn
33	1 and 2 Mc	Rv
34	Dn	"

ABBREVIATIONS OF THE
BOOKS OF THE BIBLE

Acts	Acts of the Apostles	2 Kgs	2 Kings
Am	Amos	Lam	Lamentations
Bar	Baruch	Lk	Luke
1 Chr	1 Chronicles	Lv	Leviticus
2 Chr	2 Chronicles	Mal	Malachi
Col	Colossians	1 Mc	1 Maccabees
1 Cor	1 Corinthians	2 Mc	2 Maccabees
2 Cor	2 Corinthians	Mi	Micah
Dn	Daniel	Mk	Mark
Dt	Deuteronomy	Mt	Matthew
Eccl	Ecclesiastes	Na	Nahum
Eph	Ephesians	Neh	Nehemiah
Est	Esther	Nm	Numbers
Ex	Exodus	Ob	Obadiah
Ez	Ezekiel	Phil	Philippians
Ezr	Ezra	Phlm	Philemon
Gal	Galatians	Prv	Proverbs
Gn	Genesis	Ps(s)	Psalms
Hb	Habakkuk	1 Pt	1 Peter
Heb	Hebrews	2 Pt	2 Peter
Hg	Haggai	Rom	Romans
Hos	Hosea	Ru	Ruth
Is	Isaiah	Rv	Revelation
Jas	James	Sg	Song of Songs
Jb	Job	Sir	Sirach
Jdt	Judith	1 Sm	1 Samuel
Jer	Jeremiah	2 Sm	2 Samuel
Jgs	Judges	1 Thes	1 Thessalonians
Jl	Joel	2 Thes	2 Thessalonians
Jn	John	Ti	Titus
1 Jn	1 John	1 Tm	1 Timothy
2 Jn	2 John	2 Tm	2 Timothy
3 Jn	3 John	Tb	Tobit
Jon	Jonah	Wis	Wisdom
Jos	Joshua	Zec	Zechariah
Jude	Jude	Zep	Zephaniah
1 Kgs	1 Kings		